Oxenholme

trains and train working in the heyday of BR steam — through the eyes of Alec Mayor

John Pickup

Cumbrian Railways Association

Other Cumbrian Railways Association publications

An Introduction to Cumbrian Railways *(David Joy)*

'Cumbrian Communities' Series

No 1 Grange-over-Sands *(Leslie R Gilpin)* — Out of print
No 2 Ravenglass *(Peter van Zeller)* — Out of print
No 3 Dalton-in-Furness *(Rock Battye)*
No 4 Whitehaven *(Howard Quayle)* — Out of print
No 5 Millom *(Alan Atkinson)*

'Railway Histories' Series

The Coniston Railway (second impression) *(Dr Michael Andrews & Geoff Holme)*
The Track of the Ironmasters *(W McGowan Gradon — edited by Peter Robinson)*
The Ulverstone and Lancaster Railway *(Leslie R Gilpin)*
The Pilling Pig — A History of the Garstang & Knott End Railway *(Dave Richardson)*
Bigrigg — A History of the Bigrigg branch of the Whitehaven, Cleator & Egremont Railway *(The Bigrigg Research Team)*
Kendal Tommy *(Dave Richardson)* — Out of print
Lancaster's Line to the Sea — A History of the Glasson Branch of the LNWR *(Dave Richardson)*
The Kendal and Windermere Railway (second edition) *(Dick Smith)*

Photographic Albums

A Cumbrian Railway Album *(Leslie R Gilpin)* — Out of print
A North Lancashire Railway Album *(Leslie R Gilpin)*

Books for Children

Time for Coppernob *(Denny Mallows)*

Other Titles

Railwaymen of Cumbria Remembered — A Roll of Honour

Books can be ordered *via* the Cumbrian Railways Association web site at cumbrianrailways.org.uk

Published by the Cumbrian Railways Association,
104 Durley Avenue, Pinner, Middlesex. HA5 1JH

The Association is Registered Charity No 1025436
www.cumbrianrailways.org.uk
Please see the web site for details of membership and an application form to join

Design and layout by Allan Jones
Printed by Border Offset, Rigg St, Caldewgate, Carlisle, Cumberland. CA2 5TN.

ISBN 978-1-914248-01-6

Cover image: Crewe North 'Black Five' 44763 pilots Polmadie Rebuilt Scot 4-6-0 46107 *Argyll and Sutherland Highlander* as they restart W282, the 11-00 am Glasgow Central to Manchester Victoria, from its Oxenholme stop on Saturday, 15th March 1958. CRA Mayor Collection MAY350.

Contents

	Introduction	4
1	Railways around Oxenholme	6
2	The Trains around Oxenholme	12
3	Express Passenger	15
4	Stopping Passenger Trains	33
5	Parcels and Perishables Trains	36
6	Freight Trains	38
7	A Peak Summer Saturday at Oxenholme	42
	Acknowledgements	47

A brace of LMS Jubilees 45738 *Samson* (12B Upperby) and 45601 *British Guiana* (26A Newton Heath) provide super-power hurrying C384, the 9-30 am Manchester Victoria/9-43 am Liverpool Exchange to Edinburgh and Glasgow Central through the station and onto the climb towards Grayrigg. Wednesday 10th May 1961. CRA Mayor Collection MAY349.

The Cumbrian Railways Association (CRA) is a registered charity founded in 1976. Our aims are to promote and improve the knowledge and understanding of the railways of Cumbria and their social and physical impact from when they started right up to the present day. The CRA maintains written and photographic archives of much of the railways of the region, along with associated historical events. We have over 550 members, UK and world wide, and are always keen to welcome more. For more information about the Association and membership, please visit our website at www.cumbrianrailways.org.uk .

Introduction — why this book?

This book was inspired by the enthusiasm of the late Alec Mayor for observing and recording, in photographs and notebooks, trains and train working especially around Oxenholme in the heyday of BR steam. This heyday was surely the late 1950s, when steam reached its zenith, and the early 1960s before diesel traction relegated steam locomotives to secondary status, decline and ultimate disappearance from service in 1968.

Alec Mayor was for many years a resident of Kendal and worked for the *Westmorland Gazette* as an advertising executive. His employment afforded sufficient flexibility for him to sometimes observe train working on the nearby West Coast main line several times a day at Oxenholme where he conveniently collected parcels for the 'Gazette' — and where better to do that than Oxenholme, an important junction and centre of railway operation less than three miles from his home town.

A young Alec Mayor (second from left) with father Bill Mayor and the crew of Newton Heath Jubilee 45671 *Prince Rupert*, standing in the Down Main platform at the north end of Oxenholme station. This could well be the occasion of an arranged footplate trip for Alec, probably in Spring 1955, on 45671, piloted by an LMS 2P 4-4-0 over Shap to Carlisle. CRA Mayor Collection MAY206 (See also MAY148, MAY157 and MAY168).

This publication is equally inspired and made possible by the painstaking work of the late Paul Irving on a set of Alec Mayor's notebooks covering the period from June 1957 to December 1961. These had been lodged with him by a friend of his who had providentially spotted and rescued them from oblivion during a house clearance. Paul, a career railwayman, has created from the notebooks an engaging narrative where Alec's observations are overlain with his own experiences and insights as a Carlisle train-controller during this period. This narrative has elements of both Kilvert's Diaries, being a chronological commentary on daily happenings, and War and Peace, as it runs to over 200,000 words. The compiled notebooks are being published electronically in their entirety by Cumbrian Railways Association (CRA).

Oxenholme, a busy junction station at the foot of the Westmorland fells on the West Coast main line between London and Scotland, held many fascinations for the enthusiast. There was the thrill of crack Anglo-Scottish expresses speeding south, and the awesome sight and sound of heavy trains charging, forging bravely, or just plain slogging, their way up the climb towards Grayrigg and then Shap Summit. There were slower Cumbrian expresses too that stopped at Oxenholme and characteristically gathered or scattered portions as they journeyed to and from the South. All this was interspersed with local and branch services to and from Windermere.

Paul Irving organised a number of enthusiasts' railway tours in Europe and we see him here studying timetables during a trip on the German railways.

Then there were the freights, fast freights galore, rattling through day and night, as well as slower ones still travelling long distances, and local pick-up freights tripping quietly from place to place. And there were parcels, milk, meat, fish and travelling post office trains, and the comings and goings of pilots and bankers to further spice the mix. In summer, the passenger service was swelled substantially, both by additional seasonal services and by spasmodic excursion trains to the Lakes or to the seaside.

Keeping this complex pattern of services running tolerably to the timetable was a daily challenge to the operating and control staff. In the peak holiday season, or bad weather, the challenge became immense, sometimes overwhelming, but the challenge was invariably met.

Drawing both on the compiled notebooks and on Alec's own photographs, as well as the wider image collections of the CRA and other documentary sources, this publication sets out neither to be a history, nor a comprehensive record. It seeks rather to capture, with just the necessary context, the essence of the railway scene around the busy Cumbrian junction that was Oxenholme, and some of the daily challenges and goings-on that so fascinated both Alec Mayor and Paul Irving.

Enjoy the scene, and how it changed from season to season and year to year, in those few heady years that were the heyday of BR steam.

John Pickup,
Bridgnorth, September 2022

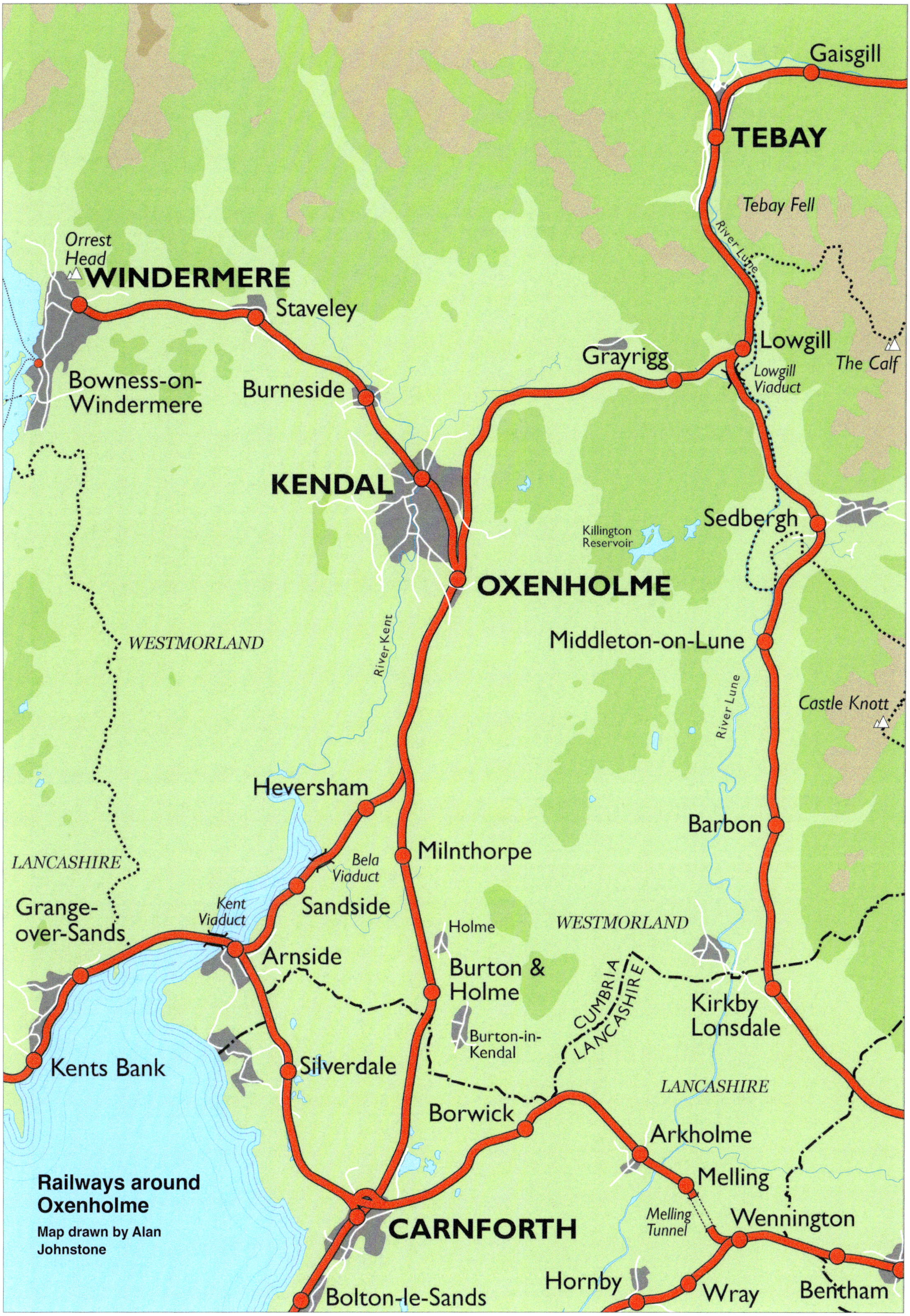
Gaisgill
TEBAY
Tebay Fell
River Lune
Orrest Head
WINDERMERE
Staveley
Lowgill
The Calf
Grayrigg
Lowgill Viaduct
Bowness-on-Windermere
Burneside
KENDAL
Sedbergh
Killington Reservoir
OXENHOLME
Middleton-on-Lune
WESTMORLAND
River Kent
Castle Knott
River Lune
Heversham
Barbon
Milnthorpe
Bela Viaduct
LANCASHIRE
Grange-over-Sands
Kent Viaduct
Sandside
Holme
WESTMORLAND
Arnside
Burton & Holme
CUMBRIA
LANCASHIRE
Kirkby Lonsdale
Burton-in-Kendal
Kents Bank
Silverdale
LANCASHIRE
Borwick
Arkholme
Melling
Railways around Oxenholme
Map drawn by Alan Johnstone
Melling Tunnel
Wennington
CARNFORTH
Hornby
Wray
Bentham
Bolton-le-Sands

1. Railways around Oxenholme

Oxenholme station and its surroundings

The south end of Oxenholme station looking north from the Old Hutton road bridge south of the station with No. 2 signal box and the small goods yard to the right. Complex pointwork connects the 'Bay' branch platform and the lines behind the station to the Up and Down Main and Down Slow. Though also connected to the Windermere branch north of the station, the lines behind the station operate as sidings and are not signalled for through traffic. CRA Irvine Collection IRV029.

The railway centre that developed at Oxenholme started life as Kendal Junction. The name tells its own story, as the chosen route for the Lancaster and Carlisle Railway focused on gaining height for the long climb over the Cumbrian hills, which ended at Shap Summit. Kendal, the most important town between Lancaster and Carlisle, was thus left to be served by a branch line that fell away downhill again, built by the Kendal and Windermere railway.

Kendal Junction station opened with the line to Kendal in September 1846, but the lines to Carlisle and Windermere soon followed – Carlisle in December 1846 and Windermere in April 1847. The name Oxenholme, by which the station became known around 1860, was taken from the farm just down the hill. Being the point at which the climb to Shap, starting near sea level at Carnforth, steepens in earnest with the 7-mile climb to Grayrigg, locomotive stabling and servicing facilities were provided to house assisting engines as well as those for local traffic, and the village of Oxenholme grew up around the railway, much of it built by the London & North Western Railway to house its employees.

The layout at Oxenholme station in BR steam days was closely similar to the original layout of 1846. The main station buildings were on the Up (east) side, while on the Down side was an island platform whose westerly face, known as the 'Bay', was connected only to the Windermere line. In the early 1880s, the platforms were substantially lengthened southwards, which involved re-routing the Kendal to Old Hutton road onto an overbridge approached by tortuous bends that remain today.

A double junction with the branch was installed immediately north of the station and a refreshment room and other facilities added on the island platform, which was later protected by a wall and overall roof. By the mid-1950s, the glazed platform canopies that once covered most of the length of the Up and Down platforms had been cut back, as happened in many places on the post-war railway, continuing to cover primarily the central sections.

There was a very small goods yard on the Up side north of the road bridge, behind Oxenholme No. 2 signal box, though it still sported a 5-ton crane and offered the full range of traffic facilities.

South of the bridge on the Down side was Oxenholme MPD, a 4-road shed with coal stage and turntable. There were two Down loops between the MPD and the main lines to hold freight trains requiring regulation, into suitable gaps in the northbound traffic for the ascent to Grayrigg summit. These loops, with a matching Up loop, stretched south to Oxenholme No. 1 signal box just north of the A65 trunk road to Skipton.

Alec Mayor took many photographs at Oxenholme. He clearly came to enjoy the friendship and confidence of railway staff, and was thus able to take pictures from the trackside, both around the junction with the Windermere branch to the north and towards the goods loops south of the road bridge.

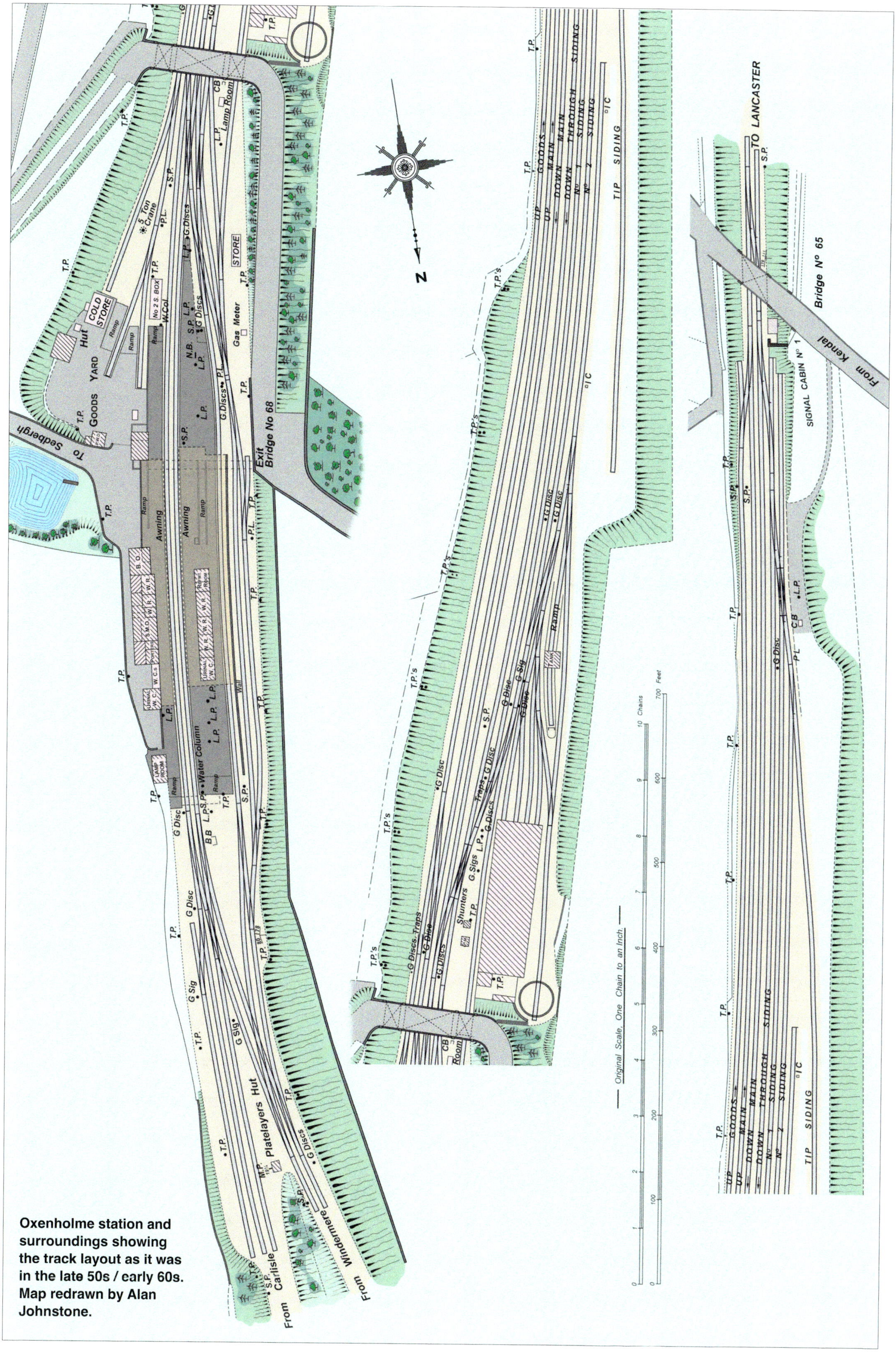

Oxenholme station and surroundings showing the track layout as it was in the late 50s / early 60s. Map redrawn by Alan Johnstone.

LMS Stanier 2-6-4T 42464, an Oxenholme loco throughout BR days until the shed's closure in June 1962 (except for three months at Stoke in Spring 1960), stands facing south outside the four-road MPD in the final days around May 1962.
CRA Irvine Collection IRV030.

Seen from Oxenholme No. 1 signal box, Stanier 8F 2-8-0 48713 (3A Bescot) charges north towards Oxenholme station and the climb to Grayrigg with a Down freight in the early to mid-1950s. Across in the Up Loop, Stanier 2-6-4T 42544 stands on five coaches of local passenger stock. Allocated to Carnforth in the early 1950s, then an Upperby loco from Feb 1955, 42544 has probably arrived on an Up local, possibly from Windermere, or maybe the 1-51 pm from Carlisle.
CRA Mayor Collection MAY096.

The platform of the Down Main home and junction signals, a favourite spot of Alec's for photography, affords a clear view of the junction and track layout to the north of the station with the main line over Shap straight ahead and the Windermere branch diverging left. Note there is no connection from the branch platform (the 'Bay') back onto the Carlisle line. Taken mid-afternoon in the winter months between November 1956 and April 1958, an unidentified LMS 'Black Five' races down from Grayrigg with an Up express of LNER stock, which could be a special or possibly W160/E509, the 12-50 pm SO Broomielaw–Manchester Victoria troop train. To the left an Up freight from the branch has arrived in the branch platform and has been banked bunker-first by an LMS 'Jinty' 0-6-0T, probably 47503, which was an Oxenholme loco until April 1958.
CRA Mayor Collection MAY177.

Oxenholme – Tebay

By the time it reached Oxenholme, the Lancaster to Carlisle line had already climbed some 250 feet in the 13 miles from Carnforth. But now the line set its sights firmly on Shap and climbed another 300 feet in the next seven miles that were Grayrigg Bank. Once clear of the station, and heading due north, the gradient steepened purposefully to 1 in 104.

Easing for less than half a mile to 1 in 213 before Peat Lane, the serious climbing resumed with more than three miles at 1 in 124, easing to 1 in 131 as it rounded Hay Fell and turned east to Docker. Here it steepened again to 1 in 106 for the final two miles past Lambrigg and Mosedale Hall Crossings to reach the summit at Grayrigg.

This was fine country for photographs, and Alec Mayor frequently found the opportunity to enjoy the sight and sound of trains battling up or hurtling down Grayrigg Bank.

While northbound expresses of the day passing Oxenholme at 60 mph or so would work hard to keep speed into the 40s up to Grayrigg, southbound expresses would race down in the 70s or even 80s, with judicious braking for the bends and the 70 mph restriction through Oxenholme at the foot of the bank.

The small station at Grayrigg had closed in February 1954, but the Up and Down loops, opened as such in 1926, were busy with freights as they were eased in and out of the constant flow of express passenger trains.

Over the next six miles, from Grayrigg to Tebay past Low Gill, junction for the Ingleton line, the line stops climbing. There's welcome respite for beleaguered firemen on northbound trains, as well as an opportunity to replenish water supplies over Dillicar troughs. Or, for those determined to climb Shap unassisted, there's the chance to get a run at the bank with its final four miles at 1 in 75, which takes the line to its summit 916 feet above sea level.

Viewed from the trackside by Docker Bridge, Princess Royal Pacific 46210 *Princess Beatrice* heads towards the magnificent snow-capped Howgill Fells as she climbs to Docker Viaduct in the distance with a Down express in the mid-1950s. CRA Mayor Collection MAY283.

Docker Viaduct, viewed from the valley below on the south side, with a Princess Royal Pacific, probably 46212 *Duchess of Kent*, climbing to Grayrigg with a Down express in the mid-1950s. CRA Mayor Collection MAY288.

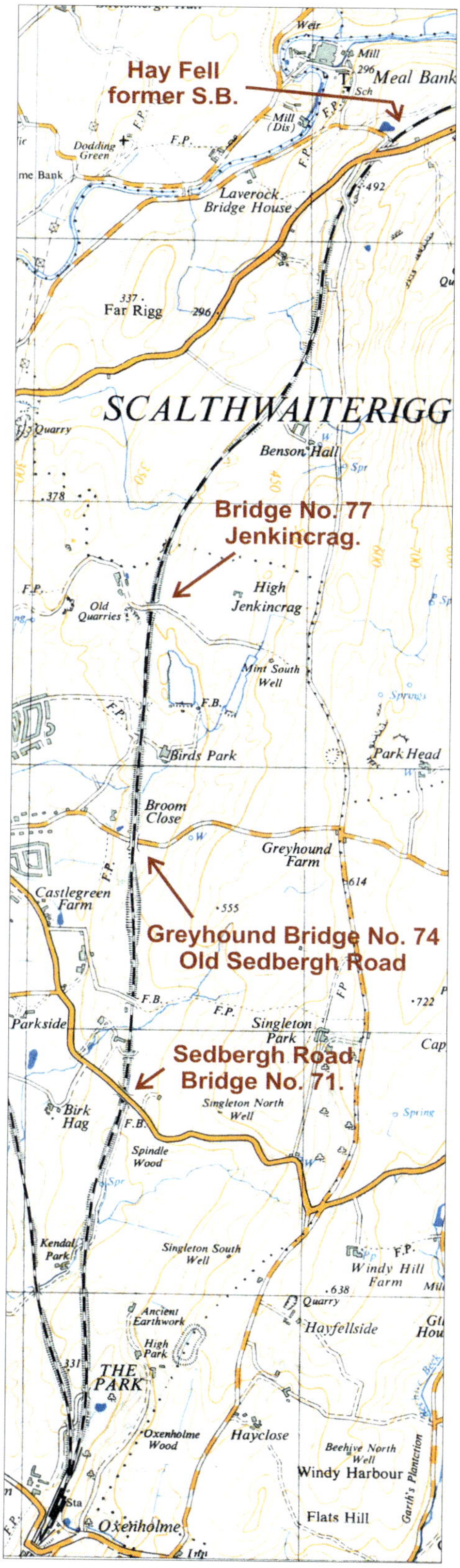

The West Coast main line from Oxenholme north to Hay Fell. OS 1:25,000 Published 1952.

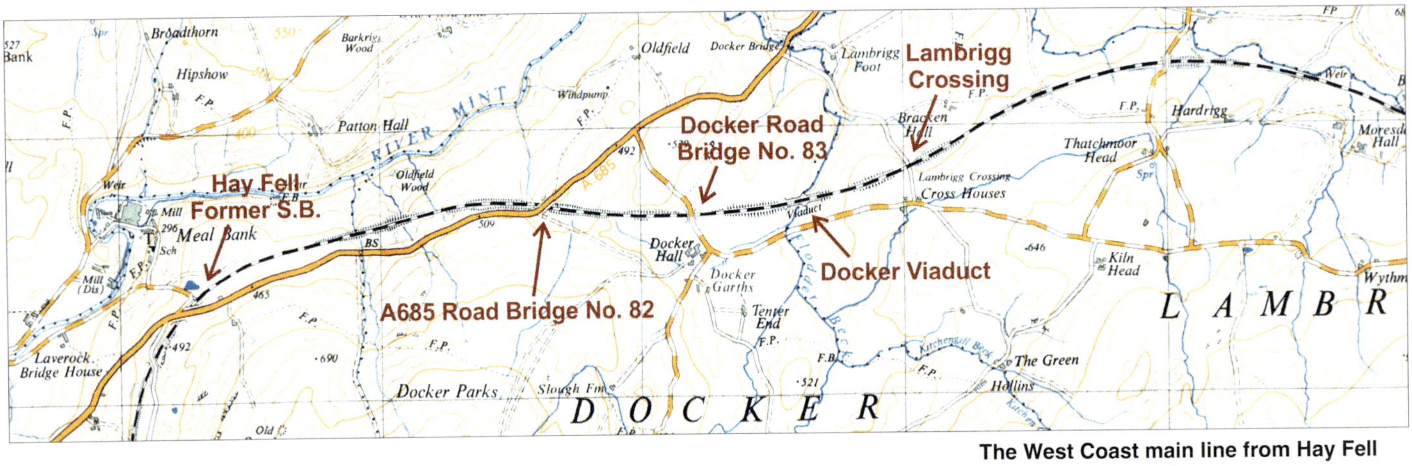

The West Coast main line from Hay Fell east towards Grayrigg.
OS 1:25,000 Published 1952.

A Stanier 'Black Five', possibly 44936 or 44939 of Upperby, crosses the junction at Low Gill with an Up evening Class E freight in the 1950s, and approaches the station leaving the Ingleton line branching off to its left. CRA Mayor Collection MAY341.

Hincaster Junction looking north towards the signal box from alongside the single-track branch to Arnside on Saturday, 24th September 1960. LMS 4F 0-6-0 44469, a Tebay loco until 1958, much used on the coke trains to and from Furness, is now a Carnforth loco heading home along the main line with the 1-50 pm Burneside–Carnforth Class K trip freight.
CRA Pearsall Collection A6032-2.

Oxenholme – Carnforth

South from Oxenholme the line to Carnforth falls continuously for the first six miles to beyond Milnthorpe. After a dead straight and level stretch for two miles to Burton & Holme, there's then a gentle climb for a mile and a half to MP 9½ (measured from Lancaster) followed by a renewed fall at 1 in 134 bringing the line close to sea level just north of Carnforth. Northbound expresses not stopping at Carnforth or Oxenholme would past Carnforth in the 70s with speed gradually falling after Milnthorpe towards 60 mph by Oxenholme. Going south with a clear road, speed could stay in the 80s all the way.

At Hincaster Junction, 3½ miles from Oxenholme, a single line branches off west to Arnside on the Carnforth–Barrow line, a route taken by the only regular mineral trains passing through Oxenholme, carrying coke from Co. Durham to the iron and steel works in Furness.

Milnthorpe, as well as a small goods yard, had a Libby's factory that despatched important traffic on the line in milk tanks and vans. At Burton & Holme, Up and Down goods loops were installed in 1925/6 like those at Grayrigg; around ¾ mile long, access was controlled by Burton & Holme No. 1 box to the south and No. 2 to the north.

Carnforth was a major rail centre in its own right, with lines branching off west to Furness and east over the ex-Midland Railway route to Leeds. There was a large motive power depot and extensive freight yards and loops.

Oxenholme – Windermere

Windermere station in the early to mid-1950s, looking north-west from the signal box, with the goods yard to the right of the passenger platforms and carriage sidings to the left. CRA Mayor Collection MAY060.

The branch to Kendal and Windermere, double track all the way in the days of steam, fell straight away from the junction at the north end of Oxenholme station at a steady 1 in 80 for the two miles to Kendal station. This had a relatively simple two-platform layout with just a trailing dock on the Down side at the Windermere end. Beyond the station there was an extensive goods and coal yard, again with a trailing connection on the Down side, and still busy into the 1960s.

Once through Kendal station, the line began an unbroken climb to the summit, which lay about a mile and a half short of Windermere station. The gradient was initially 1 in 165, but there were stretches of 1 in 80 after both Burneside (4 miles from Oxenholme) and Staveley stations (6½ miles) that gave Down local passenger trains that called there challenging restarts.

At Burneside, four miles from Oxenholme, there was a connection to a tramway leading to the paper mills of James Cropper & Company, which were a significant source of traffic, with coal and raw materials going in, and at one time paper products being shipped out in fitted vans.

For the last mile into Windermere, the line fell steeply again at 1 in 75, so Up trains starting from Windermere had a challenging start, as indeed they had leaving Kendal for the south.

However, the gradient into Windermere station did facilitate an unusual procedure for releasing engines on incoming passenger trains from their stock. Instead of employing a pilot or installing run-round facilities, arriving trains could simply be pushed back out up the hill and the stock allowed to roll back under control of the guard once the engine had moved away. Unsurprisingly, the practice was not entirely infallible, and in August 1962 descending stock overran and demolished a good part of the station end wall.

There was a modest goods yard on the Up side at Windermere with a goods shed and cattle pens as well as facilities for coal merchants.

Trains leaving Kendal for Oxenholme and the south faced a stiff climb of two miles at 1 in 80. Early on a summer morning, probably in the mid-1950s, unrebuilt Patriot 4-6-0 45548 *Lytham St Annes* of Crewe North climbs alongside Castle Road, Kendal towards Oxenholme with an Up express passenger, passing Kendal's Down distant. The angle of the sun suggests the time will be around 8-30 am and the train will be Alec's most recorded train W204, 8-10 am Windermere–Manchester, the erstwhile 'Club' train. W204 was routinely a Crewe North turn and often used for 'running-in' locos fresh out of Crewe Works. CRA Mayor Collection MAY293.

2. The Trains around Oxenholme

Passenger trains — the daily pattern

Alec Mayor, like many an enthusiast, was particularly attracted by crack express passenger trains such as the Royal Scot and, for him especially, the Caledonian. These of course were day-time trains, but the daily flow of passenger trains through Oxenholme was actually at its most intense during the night.

In the small hours, between midnight and 6 am, a flurry of sleeper trains passed through heading for the north, carrying passengers as they slept between the major cities of England and Scotland. Even in winter, there would typically be four overnight trains from Euston to Glasgow as well as trains to Inverness, Aberdeen, Perth and Stranraer. Sleeper expresses ran to Glasgow from Birmingham and Liverpool too. In summer, there were yet more.

These nocturnal expresses all pounded straight through Oxenholme and up into the hills, but shortly before 5 am an overnight train with a through-coach and passenger brake from Euston arrived and stopped at Oxenholme, before heading down the branch to Windermere, its final destination. This was the morning 'Mail'.

The corresponding southbound procession started earlier, led around 9 pm by a return overnight train from Windermere to Euston. Early evening departures from Glasgow followed before midnight, and, all being well, the southbound services from Scotland had all rushed south before 4 am.

That was it for expresses for a while; the next trains to appear with Class A lamps, the 6-10 am Carlisle–Crewe at around 7-45 am and the 6-00 am Warrington–Carlisle just after 8-30 am, were two slowcoaches of the northern West Coast mainline, stopping at almost every possible station and so averaging less than 30 mph over their journeys.

But, while the 'Warrington' was still in the station, Alec Mayor's most thoroughly recorded train appeared. This was the former 'Club' train, the 8-10 am Windermere–Manchester, which it seems Alec was regularly able to observe from his breakfast table in Kendal.

Around 10 am, the first train of the day connecting Oxenholme and the southern Lakes with Euston drew to a stand at Platform 1, on the Up Main. This was train W74, variously the 8-30 or 8-40 am Carlisle–Euston, and it was one of those expresses to and from Cumbrian destinations that characteristically gathered portions as they went south, and scattered them off again as they returned north. At Oxenholme, W74 collected a Windermere portion that had arrived in the 'Bay', normally headed by a 2-6-4 tank.

Until 1957, and the summer timetable had come into operation, there wouldn't then be another Up express coming south over Shap during the week until after 1 pm. But, on Monday, 17th June, The Caledonian, Alec's favourite express, began its seven years of high-speed, limited load running between Euston and Glasgow.

The Up Caledonian which left Glasgow at 8-30 am would tear through Oxenholme behind a Duchess Pacific around 11-15 am. Alec often contrived to be there to see it, as well as train W86, the 11-00 am from Windermere, which ran to Crewe on winter weekdays and through to Euston on Saturdays. This, in high summer, became the famous, multi-portion, Lakes Express.

Just before W86 departed south around 11-30 am, train C384, the first of the heavy expresses that connected the north-west

Just after 8-30 am on a summer's morning, Jubilee 4-6-0 45689 *Ajax* of Crewe North arrives with the 8-10 am Windermere–Manchester, the erstwhile 'Club' train, climbing off the branch towards the 'Bay'. Meanwhile, Edge Hill 'Black Five' 45187 awaits the connection before departing with the 6-00 am Warrington to Carlisle passenger on Thursday, 29th August 1963. Alec frequently used these trains when heading north for a day on the railway. CRA Tordoff collection TOR0674.

The Caledonian, behind one of Camden's finest, Coronation 4-6-2 46239 *City of Chester*, flies down from the fells, easing below the 70 mph speed limit approaching Oxenholme station around 11-15 am in 1957, the first summer of the train's operation. From Alec's notebooks the day is possibly Monday, 22nd July 1957. CRA Mayor Collection MAY182.

Around 1 pm on Friday, 20th July 1956, Camden's 46239 *City of Chester,* clears the overbridge to the west of Low Gill station with the Up Royal Scot, hauling a set of coaches pristine in the newly-introduced BR maroon livery.
CRA Pearsall Collection PEG750.

Looking south around 4-30 pm towards the station from between the Carlisle and Windermere lines, Rebuilt Patriot 4-6-0 45545 *Planet* departs towards Carlisle with a Down 7-coach express passenger, probably the Carlisle portion of W251, the weekday 10-40 am Euston–Carlisle. The detached Windermere portion would be standing in the platform out of sight ready to go forward behind a local 2-6-4T. Probably taken in the Spring or Autumn of 1957 or 1958.
CRA Mayor Collection MAY152.

cities of Manchester and Liverpool with Glasgow and Edinburgh, would pound through going north. In winter, portions from Manchester and Liverpool would be combined at Preston, and an Edinburgh portion would then be split off at Carstairs to run into Princes Street. In summer, demand was such that these trains ran in two, three or four separate parts.

Between 11-30 am and 1 pm in winter, the only express to trouble the signalmen was W27, a Crewe–Perth express with a portion for Glasgow, which stopped for a few minutes on its way north. Then between 1 pm and 3 pm, Oxenholme saw the doyen of west coast route Anglo-Scottish expresses, the Royal Scot, race through both north and south. Leaving both Euston and Glasgow at 10-00 am, the Up service was the first to appear, soon after 1 pm — Oxenholme being some 100 miles nearer to Glasgow than to London. The Down Royal Scot raced north around 2-30 pm.

Both Up and Down 'Scots' were followed at a respectful distance by heavy expresses connecting Birmingham with Glasgow and Edinburgh. In the meantime, W33, the first express of the day from London to Windermere, called shortly before 2 pm; W110, the first Perth–London express, ran south shortly after 2 pm; and W282, the counterpart of C384, with portions from Glasgow and Edinburgh for Manchester and Liverpool, called at Oxenholme before 3 pm.

From 3 pm until just after 7 pm, there were typically another ten expresses through Oxenholme. Things started in the Down direction with C400, for most of the year a modest five-coach Manchester–Carlisle train on weekdays, though extended to Glasgow on Saturdays. In summer, C400 became a fully-fledged Manchester and Liverpool to Glasgow and Edinburgh train of many portions, and on summer Saturdays it ran as two trains. In the Up direction, shortly before 4 pm, W220, an express from Windermere, went south to Preston. In the summer this went on to Liverpool Exchange, having run from there to Windermere in the morning.

Things really hotted up around 4-30 pm, and Alec Mayor often managed to appear whatever the day of the week to see what was going on. W251, the Euston–Carlisle counterpart of W74 that went Up in the morning, stopped to detach its Windermere portion.

Shortly afterwards, the veteran Midday Scot, which left Glasgow around 1-30 pm, rushed through heading south. This was followed around 5 pm by the second Perth–Euston express of the day. Not long after 5-30 pm came W128, another of these chameleon trains that was modest in winter, as a Carlisle–Preston train, but in summer started from Glasgow and Edinburgh and went to Liverpool and Manchester. It often ran in two parts on summer Saturdays.

That was it for expresses on the Up until after 8 pm, but now the Down road started to get busy. A little after 6 pm the northbound Midday Scot charged north into the hills followed equally purposefully by C402 from Manchester and Liverpool to Glasgow. Just before 7 pm, W99, a Perth express that left London right on the heels of the Midday Scot, but which shed a Blackpool portion at Preston, called at the Down platform. And, immediately after 7 pm, the erstwhile 'Club' train rolled home from Manchester, before heading down the branch taking weary businessmen back to their houses around the Lakes.

It was an hour before the next expresses appeared, and until 1957 these were: W140, the afternoon Glasgow and Edinburgh to Manchester and Liverpool service, and the return south of the morning slow train from Warrington. But from June of that year, there was the added treat of the Down Caledonian speeding through north around 8-15 pm, which frequently saw Alec back at the station to record its progress.

By 9 pm, the cycle was starting over again, with the early evening departures from Glasgow coming through, as well as the overnight Windermere–Euston express. By 9.15 pm the returning Carlisle–Crewe slowcoach had tramped off back to Carlisle.

Interleaved with all these expresses of course were stopping passenger trains, not to mention all the parcels, milk, fish and dozens of goods trains. Perhaps inevitably, Alec Mayor paid the local passenger trains much less attention with both his notebook and his camera, though in the early 1960s he took to riding them on the footplate up and down the branch with the enginemen with whom he clearly developed firm friendships. More of these trains later, but, for now, suffice it to say there were typically eight or nine stopping trains each way on the branch each day.

Most ran just between Oxenholme and Windermere, though others, including the first Up and Down trains of the day, ran through to and from Carnforth, with a few extended to Lancaster and one from Preston. There was also a local stopping train service over Shap between Carlisle and Oxenholme, with one train coming south, but two going north.

On Sundays, once Saturday's overnight trains had gone through in the early hours, little stirred until lunchtime. The Sunday service through Oxenholme was not only very limited, it was unpredictable, and subject to delay because of engineering works. The Royal Scot ran, as did the Midday Scot in summer from 1958, but they took another couple of hours on their journey. There were trains between Birmingham, Manchester, Liverpool and Glasgow, Edinburgh, and a London–Carlisle service in each direction. The Windermere branch saw only four or five trains each way. Though Alec Mayor often ventured out on Sundays, his recording, for whatever reason, was similarly curtailed. While he generally noted the locos involved, his normally assiduous recording of times and timekeeping ceased, perhaps because on Sundays they reflected primarily the indignities suffered from engineering works en route rather than the performance of man and machine that clearly so fascinated him.

The above outline of the daily pattern of scheduled passenger train services through most of the year notes how in summer increased demand led to some trains having their journeys extended, acquiring additional portions, or splitting into separate trains. But summer, especially summer Saturdays, brought scheduled trains to new destinations too, though some ran only in peak season. For example, the summer timetable introduced trains carrying holidaymakers to Blackpool from Glasgow, and from Newcastle, Darlington and South Shields over Stainmore. Regular trains ferried passengers between the Lancashire coast resorts and Windermere, and Keswick gained through trains to Manchester and London, the latter as a Workington portion of the Lakes Express. The concluding Chapter of this book is dedicated to an account of the enthralling goings-on at Oxenholme on a typical peak summer Saturday in the heyday of BR steam.

Enough for outlines: the next Chapter looks in more detail at some of the most important and characteristic of Oxenholme's passenger trains, and their operation and performance.

Camden Coronation Pacific 46239 *City of Chester* starts the serious part of the climb to Grayrigg with plenty of steam to spare, perhaps having suffered a signal check, heaven forfend, hauling the Down Afternoon Caledonian through Oxenholme around 8-15 pm on a summer's evening between 1958 and 1960. CRA Mayor Collection MAY156.

A 'Super-D' at Oxenholme! In July 1957, under the admiring gaze of fellow photographers, former LNWR G2A 0-8-0 48926 of Patricroft starts an afternoon Up Class E freight from the Windermere branch out of the 'Bay' through platform. CRA Buck Collection SBW031.

3. Express Passenger

Camden's Duchess (Princess Coronation Class) 46247 *City of Liverpool* approaches Hincaster Junction on Saturday, 24th September 1960 with the once iconic 10 o'clock. Electrification works further south, as BR battled to run a railway while rebuilding it at the same time, mean W63, the Down Royal Scot, is now the 9-05 am Euston–Glasgow, and slimmed down to a mere seven passenger coaches plus a Full Brake (BG) to maintain a semblance of a competitive schedule. CRA Pearsall Collection A6032-6.

During the five short years from 1957, when Alec Mayor began his detailed recording, to when his records end in 1961, the service of express passenger trains on the West Coast main line changed more than it had since the 1930s, excluding the war years of course. Initially there was still improvement, for example with the addition of The Caledonian as a high-speed service from June 1957. In his compilation of Alec Mayor's notebooks, Paul Irving describes Summer 1958 as the 'high summer of steam' on the line, but from then it was all downhill. He describes as 'seismic' the changes introduced with the Winter 1958/9 timetable, which saw 15 minutes added to journey times between London and the North as preparations for electrification got underway.

To minimise disturbance at the hub of the system that was Crewe, most Down trains were simply timed to start ten minutes earlier from Euston and arrive at their destinations about five minutes later. So horror of horrors, the iconic 10-00 am Euston–Glasgow Royal Scot suddenly became the 9-50! Going south, 15 minutes of 'recovery time' was added in lumps of three or four minutes here and there.

There was a slight re-acceleration for the 1959 Summer Timetable, and a hiatus as this rolled over until November because a printing strike meant no new timetable could be communicated to the travelling public. When the Winter Timetable finally appeared, 25 minutes had been added to most services south of Crewe, though the Royal Scot and Midday Scot were spared such indignity by reducing their formation to eight coaches, like the Caledonian.

In Summer 1960, the 'Scots' stayed as eight coaches on weekdays, but on Saturdays and Sundays had to load to 16 coaches or more to cope with demand. The consequence was that the Up Saturday Royal Scot didn't reach Euston until 6-35 pm, as opposed to 5-15 pm on weekdays. On Sundays, with engineering work everywhere, it was 8-25 pm before the 'Up Scot' reached Euston — all being well of course.

To quote Paul Irving again, 'unbelievably the Winter Timetable for 1960/1 made things even worse . . . despite the 35 minutes or so deceleration since 1957, a further ten minutes was added to most services between Weaver Junction and Euston'. By the time the 1961 Summer Timetable came in, the 10-00 am London–Glasgow Royal Scot had become the 9-15 am, though, to be fair, on weekdays it did take just 15 minutes longer to complete the journey than in 1957.

Fortunately, in recording the time-keeping of passenger trains, Alec Mayor also routinely noted this as minutes early or late against the timetable, whatever that happened to be at the time, so taking stock of the performance of specific trains against schedule in the following sections becomes very much easier.

Sadly, the assessments of timekeeping of selected trains that follow show that if Summer 1958 was due to be BR steam's 'high summer' as regards advertised services and schedules, in terms of punctuality it certainly wasn't.

London – Glasgow

The Royal Scot

Leaving Euston and Glasgow Central at 10-00 am, the 'Scot' was the prestige West Coast express since its introduction in 1927. In June 1957, when Alec Mayor's recording began, the Royal Scot was still a majestic 13-coach train running from Euston to Glasgow, non-stop as far as passengers were concerned, in 7¼ hours for the 400 mile journey. Making only a brief scheduled stop at Kingmoor to change crew, if running to time the Down train would roar through Oxenholme at 2-14 pm on weekdays, though not until 2-41 pm on Saturdays.

In 1957, the 'Scot' was regularly in the hands of the pioneer diesels: the Down train (W63) was most often double-headed by the LMS 'Twins', 10000 and 10001, with the Bulleid pair 10201 and 10202 often having the 'Up Scot' (W96). Sometimes the diesels would return hauling overnight trains and complete 800 miles per day — great utilisation! Alec most often recorded the Royal Scot on Saturdays, and, between June 1957 and early March 1958, the LMS diesels were in charge of the 'Down Scot' about 60% of the time. Duchesses (almost always from Camden) had charge of about 30%, and the Bulleid diesels the rest.

The LMS diesels then went missing from Alec's notebooks for three months, with Camden Duchesses again hauling the Royal Scot. The diesels reappeared for a month in July 1958, but from then on they appeared only spasmodically, and

Pioneer LMS Diesels 10000 and 10001 climb towards Bridge No. 83 at Docker running about 5 minutes late at 2-45 pm with the Down Royal Scot express passenger on Saturday, 19th October 1957. CRA Mayor Collection MAY174.

In the winter months between February 1957 and November 1959, Bulleid SR Diesels 10201 and 10202 approach Oxenholme junction from the north with the Up Royal Scot. CRA Mayor Collection MAY173.

Princess Royal 4-6-2 46209 *Princess Beatrice* (5A Crewe North) approaches Oxenholme passing the tall lattice-post Up Home signal with the Up Midday Scot express passenger. Typically, a milk tank or two has been attached to the rear. Taken in the winter months between late 1956 and early 1958.
CRA Mayor Collection MAY179.

by November 1959 both the LMS and SR diesels had been reallocated to Willesden and their time on front line expresses was over. So the Duchesses were in charge again as the 'Scot' was decelerated from September 1958, and the following year became just an eight-coach train on weekdays, until the new English Electric Type 4 diesels took over from early 1961.

Over the whole period from June 1957–December 1961, Alec's records suggest that the timekeeping of the Down Royal Scot passing Oxenholme wasn't by any means exemplary. His observations were spasmodic and by no means a complete or representative sample, but the 'Down Scot' was on time or early on just 34% of the 100 or so occasions when he recorded it, and 16% up to five minutes late. So half the time it was over five minutes down, 31% being over ten minutes down, and 11% of runs were more than 20 minutes behind time. Interestingly, Saturdays were somewhat better than weekdays, with Oxenholme being passed on time or early on 38% of the runs compared to only 20% on weekdays. The 'Up Scot' was over 15 minutes late 35% of the times he recorded it.

Among Alec's sightings there were a few occasions when the diagrammed motive power had been substituted. On Saturday, 9th May 1959, for example, the 'Down Scot' was in the hands of Rebuilt Scot 46157 *The Royal Artilleryman* of Crewe North, piloted by Upperby 'Black Five' 45295, though they were creditably only six minutes down passing Oxenholme. On Saturday, 2nd April 1960, Rebuilt Scot 46135 *The East Lancashire Regiment* had the Down train alone, and was perhaps unsurprisingly 37 minutes late.

The Midday Scot

Although the Midday Scot was launched as a titled train in 1927, like the Royal Scot, its origins go back into the 19th century and the 2 pm 'Corridor' express of LNWR days between Euston and Glasgow.

The canonical departure time of the Midday Scot was 1-30 pm and Alec Mayor frequently appeared at Oxenholme station to see the Up train go through just after 4-30 pm, weekdays and weekends alike — time for a cup of tea perhaps? He recorded the Up train on over 200 occasions between June 1957 and December 1961, and for the first three years, excluding Sundays when a 7P was frequently used, the loco was always a Pacific. More than 80% of the time this was one from Crewe North, with only spasmodic appearances by Upperby or Camden locos.

Until mid-1958, Princess Royals and Duchesses were equally likely to appear, but that quickly changed and when Polmadie's 46201 *Princess Elizabeth* flew through three minutes late on Saturday, 13th September 1958 that was to be the last Princess Royal Alec would record on this duty. Duchesses then held sway, though by the beginning of 1960 Camden locos had become the most frequent power. By the end of 1960, English Electric Type 4 diesels had started to appear, and from February 1961 onwards they had the monopoly.

The Down Midday Scot had 100 miles more to cover than the Up train before reaching Oxenholme, so it was another 100 or so minutes, generally past 6 pm, before it was due. Alec recorded the Down train less frequently but, like the Up train, Crewe North Pacifics were the customary motive power. From mid-1957 through 1959, of nearly 60 sightings only five, all Duchesses, were from elsewhere. Unlike the Up train though, Princess Royals were uncommon, appearing only four times, all before mid-1958. Again, like the Up train, 1960 saw Duchesses from other sheds, primarily Camden, take over, and in 1961 every one of Alec's sightings was an English Electric Type 4.

If the timekeeping of the Royal Scot passing Oxenholme was less than impressive over the period of Alec's records, the Midday Scot was no better. The Up and Down trains ran right time or better on just 33% and 27% of occasions, and more than 20 minutes late on 9% and 13% respectively. For the Up train things were rather worse on weekdays, though fewer trains were over 20 late. The Down was the opposite, marginally more right time or better on weekdays, but more were seriously late.

The records afford an interesting perspective on how things changed over time, at least as regards punctuality bearing in mind a succession of changes in loading and number of stops, and latterly engineering works.

In Summer 1957, the Down train had a poor time of it, always being more than five minutes late and on average 15 minutes late. Monday 3rd February 1958 saw one of those occasions when things go seriously awry. In the words of Paul Irving, *"Black Five' 45371 found itself, unusually, in charge of W97, the Down Midday Scot, from Oxenholme. The original loco, 46230 Duchess of Buccleuch, had failed with a hot axle box on the tender's leading RHS wheel set. Presumably the train had been in the Down loop, waiting for 45371 from Carnforth. W97 eventually passed through, three hours late at 9-05 pm. Doubtless the 'Black Five' would be replaced at Carlisle, by a 7P or 8P off Kingmoor!"*

After that, between March and May 1958, W97 was suddenly right time or early every time Alec recorded it. Then came the summer timetable, and the problems were back with the train running more than five minutes late on 80% of occasions, and more than ten minutes late on 63% of the runs. Winter 1958/9 saw some improvement with nearly half the trains less than five minutes late, though only 15% were right time or better. Summer 1959 saw real progress with 42% of runs now right time or better, though 25% were still more than 20 minutes late. And in Winter 1959/60, while steam still ruled and loads were reduced to eight coaches to allow acceleration back to a 7¼ hour journey time, more than half were on time or early and no train Alec recorded was more than 20 minutes late.

W126, the Up Midday Scot, was a little more punctual passing Oxenholme than the Down train, though that should surely be the case since the Down had covered 100 miles more and navigated many more busy traffic centres. Alec Mayor did not record the Up train until late 1957, as earlier in the year the departure from Glasgow wasn't until 3 pm, more of an afternoon Scot really, so it wouldn't pass Oxenholme until after 6 pm.

For the rest of the Winter 1957/8 timetable, timekeeping was grim. Only 18% of runs were right time or early and 60% were more than five minutes late. What's more, nearly 40% were more than ten minutes late after what should surely be a straightforward run from Glasgow. Summer 1958 was only marginally better, with only 48% of trains more than five minutes late, but still only 18% managed to be on time or early. As with the Down Midday, there was a real improvement during the Winter of 1958/9, and now 53% of runs were on or ahead of schedule by Oxenholme. Punctuality slipped a little in Summer 1959, perhaps unsurprisingly given those hectic summer Saturdays, but over the 1959/60 Winter timetable period 60% of runs were right time or early passing Oxenholme.

So what had changed in the Winter of 1958? The scheduled journey time from Glasgow to passing Oxenholme was still just over three hours, all the deceleration happening further south. There was no substantial change in loading, unless there

A Barrow tank on the Midday Scot no less! Fowler 2-6-4T 42364 has been recruited to assist Crewe North Coronation Pacific 46252 *City of Leicester* as they climb into the hills approaching the Sedbergh Road bridge north of Oxenholme with the Down train W97 on Saturday, 30th July 1955. Both seem to be going well, the drivers' jaws firmly set and 46252 showing a white feather to boot. Maybe the load was prodigious being the end of the Glasgow Fair holidays, for the W143 relief to the Down Midday was running that day too? CRA Pearsall Collection PEG539.

An LMS Coronation Pacific still fitted with a 'semi' sloping smokebox, races down from Docker Viaduct, visible on the far left, towards bridge No. 83 with the Up Midday Scot in the early to mid 1950s. The loco could well be 46243 *City of Lancaster*, the last Coronation to lose the semi smokebox, or possibly 46246 *City of Manchester* or 46248 *City of Leeds*. CRA Mayor Collection MAY280.

were some unrecorded change in practice around adding strengthening coaches or tail traffic perhaps? The locos were still Crewe North Pacifics, and, although the Princess Royals gradually disappeared from the Midday Scot by September 1958, their average timekeeping over that period was only two minutes worse than the Duchesses that replaced them. If the locos really were a key factor, maybe the critical point is that in the twelve months before the Princess Royals departed, the Duchesses had maintained or improved on the schedule 25% of the time: the Princess Royals, in the shape of 46201 *Princess Elizabeth* of Polmadie on Saturday, 6th September 1958, managed that only once.

The Caledonian

In June 1957, the Caledonian express was introduced as a fast, limited capacity, weekdays-only service between the two cities to respond to increasing competition from air travel. The 'Caley' ran Up to London in the morning and Down to Glasgow in the afternoon, following the successful pattern established with the Talisman on the East Coast Main Line.

The Up train left Glasgow at 8-30 am while the Down left Euston at 4-15 pm. The journey time with the eight-coach load was 6 hours 40 minutes. While this was faster than the 'Scots', it was noted to be less ambitious than the pre-war Coronation Scot which was allowed ten minutes less with a coach more, albeit with a streamlined loco and stock, though it's debatable whether that feature made a significant contribution.

Both Up and Down trains had but a single stop, at Carlisle, and both were allowed 291 minutes for the 299.1 mile trip, giving an average speed for that leg of 61.7 mph — an addition to the prestigious list of trains with faster than a mile-a-minute schedules. The Up train was scheduled to race down the hill through Oxenholme at 11-16 am, about 2¾ hours after leaving Glasgow Central. This was a time-honoured moment in the day that drew Alec Mayor to record its passing on nearly 300 occasions over four and a half years. It remained the due time throughout, except under the Summer timetable of 1959 when an extra minute was allowed, apparently because of speed restrictions over the Esk Viaduct between Carlisle and Gretna while it was being rebuilt. If only the train's timekeeping were such that the extra minute would make a noticeable difference to punctuality!

The Down train was due to climb through, somewhat more slowly given the gradient, initially at 8-14 pm, and Alec turned out in all seasons to see it over 200 times before the end of 1961. The due time moved rather more after September 1958 when the progressive decelerations for engineering preparations for electrification began, though even so it ranged only from 8-13 to 8-19 pm as departure from Euston was repeatedly moved forward. By 1962, no less than 45 minutes had been added to the journey times of both Up and Down trains. So 6 hours 40 had become 7 hours 25, though stops had been added at Stafford for both trains and at Preston for the Up train to try to boost declining patronage.

Camden Coronation Pacific 46245 *City of London* speeds down from Lambrigg towards Bridge 83 at Docker with the Up morning Caledonian, probably in early Spring 1958 or 1959, between 46245 acquiring maroon livery and being fitted with AWS in September 1959. CRA Mayor Collection MAY359.

From the first day, Monday, 17th June 1957, when Camden's 46229 *Duchess of Hamilton* and 46242 *City of Glasgow* sped the first Caledonian passengers south and north respectively, the Caledonians were naturally provided with the pride of the line, the Duchesses, to haul them. The locomotives worked through between London and Glasgow with no pause for an engine change, and for the first two years and more the trains were entrusted to Camden Duchesses. The inaugural pair, 46229 and 46242, made many repeat appearances. Alec's notebooks suggest 46239 *City of Chester* and 46245 *City of London* were particular favourites for the job which involved running north with the Down train in the afternoon, overnighting on Polmadie, and returning at the head of the Up train the following morning.

The optimism of Summer 1958, arguably the post-war zenith of West Coast main line steam, saw two additional Caledonian trains added to the timetable, again following a similar initiative with the Talisman, Down to Glasgow at 7-45 am from Euston and back Up to London at 4-00 pm. When the additional trains were introduced in Summer 1958, it was Polmadie's turn to provide the power. The first Down morning train left Euston behind 46224 *Princess Alexandra* while sister 46232 *Duchess of Montrose* took the first Up afternoon Caledonian south. These two

When the two additional daily Caledonians were introduced for their one and only summer in 1958, they were entrusted to Polmadie Duchesses, and 46224 *Princess Alexandra* with her blue-backed smokebox numberplate headed the first Down morning 'Caley'. It's possible that's the train Alec has photographed here, charging north through Oxenholme 3 minutes behind schedule at 11-52 am on Monday, 9th June. CRA Mayor Collection MAY128.

together with Polmadie's 46223 *Princess Alice* and 46231 *Duchess of Atholl* hauled almost all the additional summer 'Caleys'.

One notable exception, however, occurred on Monday, 7th July 1958, thanks to a derailment of some coaches at Oxenholme of all places. This led to the Up afternoon 'Caley' being diverted *via* Hellifield with Upperby Jubilee 45593 *Kolhapur* asked to take over from Carlisle — perhaps through to Euston as it was only an eight-coach load.

There were additional stops at Crewe going north and Stafford returning south, but business was insufficiently brisk and Friday, 15th September 1958 saw these extra trains run for the last time. Alec travelled up to Glasgow to ride back to Carlisle on the final Up afternoon Caledonian behind Polmadie's 46223 *Princess Alice*. His notebooks contain a log of the run that saw Gretna Junction reached uneventfully on time at 5-38 pm, but the 15 mph temporary speed restriction over the Esk Viaduct, which was being rebuilt, led to a four minutes late arrival in Carlisle.

When the winter timetable was eventually introduced in November 1959, delayed two months by a printers' strike, things changed and the provision of Duchesses for the established Caledonians became Upperby's responsibility. When the Caledonian was introduced in June 1957, Upperby had but four Duchesses, though this was significantly strengthened to nine in June 1958, slimming back to seven for that Winter. Now Upperby's fleet was boosted to eleven. The Upperby Duchesses worked overnight to Euston, taking over W224, the 10-25 pm Glasgow Central–Euston, at Carlisle No. 12 signal box and then took the Down and Up 'Caleys' to Glasgow and back in turn, as the Camden locos had done previously. They returned on the third day to Upperby in charge as far as Carlisle of W21, the 11-40 pm Euston–Glasgow St Enoch sleeper, which rejoiced in the splendid, if informal soubriquet, the 'First Porridge'. (For the record, the 'Second Porridge' was W5, the 12-10 am Euston to Glasgow Central *via* Beattock.)

And so things stayed for Alec until, on Wednesday, 1st February 1961, he first saw the Caledonian appear behind a diesel — D301, an English Electric Type 4, heading the Up train. Over the next two months Alec noted Duchesses just twice on the 'Caley', and after mid-April 1961, when seven of Upperby's Duchesses transferred to Kingmoor for duties to points north, he never recorded another.

The timekeeping of the Caledonian over the period of Alec's notes was happily much better than that of the 'Scots', more than 60% of his sightings being right time or early and fewer than 20% more than five minutes late. But as a crack, eight-coach train provided with 8P power when the 'Scots' often had half as many coaches again making recovery from delays much harder, so should it have been.

Timekeeping varied markedly though over the years and the seasons. For the first summer the two 'Caleys' did just average over 60% right time or early. But during the following winter, before the decelerations had begun, both Up and Down trains slipped to around 50%, with around 30% more than five minutes late. Summer 1958, with two trains each way, saw the established Up morning 'Caley' on top form, 88% right time or early, though the afternoon Down still hovered at 64%, now with more than 20% more than five minutes late.

Winter 1958/9 saw the Up train slump back towards 50% right time or early, though interestingly the Down improved to over 70%. And the following summer the Up could manage no better than 59% while the Down excelled itself at 87% right time or early, potentially much more significant in terms of on time arrival at Carlisle whereas the Up train had several hours of running left in which to claw lost time back. The nadir for the Up train seems to have been the period of the phoney still-Summer timetable in Autumn 1959 when Alec saw not a single train go through on time, and more than half were over ten minutes late. Then, the proud Cumbrian might claim, it was Upperby to the rescue: from November through to Junc 1960 the Up train suddenly shot back up to appear 83% right time or early at Oxenholme.

As for the two additional Caledonians launched in Summer 1958 to win business,

Sparkling clean Polmadie Duchess 46223 *Princess Alice* accelerates the last ever Up afternoon Caledonian, 4-00 pm from Glasgow Central, south from Carlisle up the 1 in 131 approaching the former station at Brisco on Friday, 12th September 1958. Alec had been on the footplate of 46223 from Glasgow Central to Carlisle. It's interesting that two of the eight coaches of this crack BR express are LMS vehicles, the leading Brake First Corridor (BFK) and the Restaurant Car.
CRA Leslie Collection LES0648. By kind permission of Peter J Robinson.

In the depths of winter between late 1962 and early 1964, an English Electric Type 4 diesel crosses Greyhound Bridge on the descent from Hay Fell to Oxenholme with the Up Caledonian. The split headcode boxes mark the loco as one of the series between D325 and D344, all of which were initially allocated to depots in the LMR Western Division. CRA Mayor Collection MAY352.

Coronation 4-6-2 46239 *City of Chester* (1B Camden) speeds the Down Caledonian express passenger north across the high embankment near Sedgwick, south of Oxenholme, around 8 pm during the first year of the train's operation.
CRA Mayor collection MAY093.

their average performance judging by Alec's observations ranged from below par to dismal. The Up afternoon train managed less than 60% right time or early at Oxenholme whereas the Down morning train managed that barely a third of the time, with almost a third of runs having more than five minutes to recover for to reach Carlisle on time.

But you know what they say about statistics! Interestingly, the railway press of the day provides a different, but by no means incompatible perspective. What was possible, given an orchestrated clear run, a speed merchant driver and possibly a specially prepared engine was illustrated on Thursday, 5th September 1957 when Driver Starvis of Camden brought the Up morning Caledonian from Glasgow to Euston in just three minutes over six hours, a post-war record, compared to the 6h 40m schedule. The loco was Camden's 46244 *King George VI* suddenly substituting for that shed's very capable 46242 *City of Glasgow*. A commentary on the run by Cecil J Allen among others appears in the *Railway Magazine*, November 1957.

The following year, in the September 1958 edition, Cecil J Allen returned to report on the running of the two additional Caledonians run that Summer. They didn't start well: both the Down morning and Up afternoon were three minutes late through Oxenholme, but it was the Up train that particularly disgraced itself. After leaving Stafford already 16½ minutes late, another 11 minutes were dropped to Euston despite minimal interference from Permanent Way slacks or signals.

Cecil J Allen, commenting that nine times of out ten the quality of running is down to the driver, seemed clear where the blame lay. Although one cannot rule out some unfortunate fault on the loco, 46232 *Duchess of Montrose*, that was rectified at Camden overnight, the lady was in quite sparkling form on the morning run back to Glasgow the following day. Heading north after the Crewe stop, 46232 was twice brought to a dead stand by signals, first at Oxheys north of Preston, and again approaching Carnforth, which was consequently passed at just 35 mph, over six minutes late. From here on in, an enterprising crew, probably Upperby men, showed what they and the Duchess could do, albeit with the routinely light load. 46232 charged through Oxenholme at 65 mph and climbed to Grayrigg summit without speed falling below 59 mph. Then the real fireworks started: the Caledonian shot through Tebay at a full 80 mph and topped Shap summit at almost 55 mph, now back on time having completed the 5½ mile climb at over a mile-a-minute.

Even so, it took a rapid descent with 87 mph at Plumpton to reach Carlisle on time, given a crawl under signals into the city that was seemingly routine at that time such that the last 1.4 miles from Carlisle No. 13 box took more than three minutes. That, and a similar run with Polmadie's 46231 *Duchess of Atholl* showed what was possible, but how often would the one-in-three Down morning Caledonians that passed Oxenholme over five minutes late manage to get the time back by Carlisle?

Birmingham – Glasgow & Edinburgh

Hard on the heels of the Royal Scot, both northbound and southbound, there followed expresses connecting Birmingham with Glasgow and Edinburgh. The Up train, W98, left Glasgow straight after the 'Scot', typically at five minutes past ten when the 'Up Scot' departed at 10-00 am. In Summer 1957 for example, when the 'Down Scot' left Euston also at ten in the morning, W67 Birmingham–Glasgow left New Street at 11-20 am, calling at Wolverhampton and dropping into place to follow in the 'Scot's' wake from Stafford northwards, stopping only at Crewe before Carlisle.

During the winter timetable period, between Crewe and Carlisle, W67 was a heavy train of 13 to 15 vehicles serving both Scottish cities, typically comprising a seven-coach portion for Glasgow followed by four coaches for Edinburgh, detached at Carstairs. In the late 1950s, W67 also brought north a three-coach portion from Euston to Perth that the preceding 'Scot' had casually discarded at Crewe. In the early 1960s, the winter train still ran to 13 or 14 vehicles, but the Perth portion had been replaced by a couple of Full Brakes (BGs). There was one from Euston and one from Marylebone, and on Mondays to Thursdays an RIR (Refrigerator Van without Gangways) from Dudley Port was attached at Wolverhampton – it must surely have been one of the Palethorpe's Sausage Vans.

In summer, Glasgow and Edinburgh were served by separate trains, W211, the 11-25 am Birmingham–Edinburgh Princes Street, following right behind W67 for Glasgow. So, on weekdays, W67 was a lighter nine- to eleven-coach train but swelled gradually to 14 coaches during the peak weeks of the summer.

W67 would power its way through Oxenholme around 2-30 to 2-45 pm, depending on the season. As Alec's observations were mostly on Saturdays when free from his desk, it was normally a heavy train that he witnessed. W67 was consistently diagrammed for 8P power, but, in contrast to the 'Scot', Princess Royals featured frequently alongside the Duchesses. Rebuilt Scots deputised on only a handful of occasions, perhaps with a pilot, and the Birmingham trains came late to dieselisation, Alec's first and only record in the period being the appearance of D330 at Tebay one April Saturday. Alec's observations show that during the late 1950s, Polmadie routinely provided the power in summer, while Crewe North took over the responsibility in winter.

Constrained to follow in the wake of the 'Down Scot', one would expect W67's timekeeping to be no better, and probably worse, than the train in front. But Alec's observations suggest otherwise, at least as measured passing Oxenholme or Tebay, with W67 more often right time or early than compared with the 'Scot', though the Birmingham train was more than 20 minutes late more often. Unsurprisingly, as most of Alec's sightings were on Saturdays, timekeeping in winter was better than in summer. In Summer 1958,

Coronation 4-6-2 46225 *Duchess of Gloucester* (5A Crewe North) approaches the road bridge at Docker (No. 83) with W67, the 11-15 am Birmingham to Glasgow express passenger in the mid- to late-1950s. CRA Mayor Collection MAY306.

The *Princess Royal* herself, No. 46200, approaches Oxenholme junction from the north with an Up express passenger; it has all the hallmarks of W98, the 10-05 am Glasgow Central–Birmingham, including an odd milk tank on the rear doubtless attached at Carlisle. From Alec's notebooks this could well be Monday, 22nd July 1957 when for a few months 46200 was on the books of Crewe North, which routinely provided the power for W98. And there's washing on the line at High Park, the large house on the hill above the loco! CRA Mayor Collection MAY176.

W67 only reached Oxenholme on time once in every four times Alec recorded it, whilst the following winter it passed right time or early on almost 60% of occasions.

The southbound Glasgow–Birmingham train, W98, mirrored the northbound service in many ways. In the summer timetable period from 1957 to 1961, W98 loaded similarly to nine to eleven bogies on weekdays, and up to 14 on peak Saturdays, Edinburgh being served by a separate train running dutifully behind — W156, the 10-10 am Edinburgh Princes Street to Birmingham. There was an interesting difference though in that in most years there was a Plymouth portion comprising up to three coaches of Western Region stock that was detached at Crewe. In some summers there was even a separate Glasgow–Plymouth train running on Fridays only.

In winter, W98 like W67 was a heavy train as it served both Scottish cities, with a four-coach Edinburgh portion being attached at Carstairs to the seven coaches from Glasgow for Birmingham, and one or two coaches for Plymouth. To add to the excitement, a loaded milk tank was often attached to the rear at Carlisle to be toted south.

Like W67, W98 was an 8P duty, and again Princess Royals were frequent performers,

Looking north from Greyhound Bridge (No. 74), up to the overbridge No. 77 at Jenkincrag, with Bird's Park Farm on the right. Princess Royal Pacific 46201 *Princess Elizabeth* (5A Crewe North) races down towards Oxenholme with the 10-05 am Glasgow–Birmingham express. The first coach is a WR Brake Composite Gangwayed (BCK) still in crimson and cream livery, which was a through-coach to Plymouth detached at Crewe. Taken between 1957 and July 1958 when 46201 moved to Polmadie. CRA Mayor Collection MAY353.

almost as frequent as the Duchesses. But Crewe North normally provided the locos both winter and summer, and until October 1961, when a free-for-all seemed to break out, more than three quarters of the trains Alec recorded had a 5A 8P on the front. Polmadie merely filled in the gaps, including with the odd Scot and Britannia when an 8P seemed not to be available.

As for timekeeping, though Oxenholme was less than 150 miles from Glasgow, W98 seemed to run seriously late more often than any other train Alec recorded. Of his sightings from Summer 1957 through Summer 1960, no less than 60% of trains were more than 20 minutes late passing Oxenholme, and they averaged 40 minutes late. This seems so odd perhaps another explanation is likely. I rather suspect we are seeing 'selection bias' in these admittedly small-number statistics, in that Alec's schedules seemed to be such that often he would only see W98, which was frequently the first afternoon train he recorded, *if* it was running pretty late.

London – Perth

Just as there were several services each day year-round between London and Glasgow/Edinburgh, there was more than a single train each way connecting London with Perth, excepting Sundays. That said, the daytime service was somewhat asymmetrical. Going south, there were two trains running through from Perth to Euston each day — W110 leaving Perth at around 9-00 am and W484 around 12-15 pm. Going north there was just one train from London to Perth, W99, which typically left Euston at 1-35 pm. But in addition there was W27, the 9-25 am Crewe–Perth, and also W65, running every day as the 4-20 pm Carlisle–Perth but which had a timetabled 'Q' path so it could be extended back to London as and when required.

Alec Mayor observed W484, the 'afternoon' Perth–London, rather more often than W110, the morning departure, so the former will serve rather better, along with W99 northbound, as an example of the southbound service.

W99 1-35 pm Euston–Perth

W99 left Euston as a substantial train typically of around twelve coaches, though 14 on a Friday, but it morphed on its way north. In Winter 1957/8 for example, the first transformation happened at Crewe where W99 shed the rear four or five coaches as a Blackpool portion which went forward as part of the 4-40 pm Crewe–Blackpool Central.

So, from Crewe to Carlisle, W99 was a relatively modest eight- or nine-coach train, but it was important in serving Cumbrian and North Lancs travellers by calling at Preston, Lancaster, Carnforth, Oxenholme and Penrith. Naturally, when W99 called at Oxenholme just before 7-00 pm there was a connecting branch passenger for Windermere waiting. At Carlisle, W99 detached a coach (or two on Fridays) and attached two parcels BGs, thus heading to Perth in a quite different shape to that which left Euston.

The formation of W99 remained broadly similar over the years of Alec's observations, but in Summer 1960, from Monday through Thursday, it additionally picked up a four-coach portion at Crewe off the 8-00 am from Plymouth. Thus it remained a heavy 14-coach train as it journeyed north through Cumbria. This Plymouth portion was destined for Glasgow and was detached at Carlisle to go forward as the 8-20 pm to Glasgow Central. On Fridays this one Summer, W99 comprised only a six-coach Glasgow portion in front of a nine-coach Perth portion. The Blackpool portion ran as a separate twelve-coach train. Then on Saturdays it was back to a Perth and Blackpool formation for W99, with no Plymouth coaches to collect at Crewe, and the Glasgow portion now running as a separate train — such complexity, just to cater for the fluctuating demands of the travelling public!

Motive power for W99 was routinely provided by Upperby, with Crewe North and Camden locos appearing spasmodically on perhaps a quarter of Alec's sightings. They never took over, their appearances being most frequent between March and June 1959 when they accounted for half of Alec's sightings of W99. There were the usual few strays such as Holbeck's 46117 on 23rd August 1957.

Even though W99 was normally an eight- or nine-coach train north of Crewe, Pacifics were used on one in three occasions, just as much before Summer 1958, when Upperby became Duchess-rich, as afterwards. The rest of Alec's 90 or so sightings were 7Ps, though Type 4 diesels appeared in November 1959 and then accounted for around 60% of sightings. In contrast to many heavier trains, Jubilees appeared only a couple of times and 'Black Fives' were completely absent.

For a train of modest length, time-keeping to Oxenholme was pretty poor, and in the first year of Alec's records it was simply gruesome. From June 1957 until the end of the summer timetable in September 1958, barely 20% of trains managed to reach Oxenholme on time. And for the last twelve of these months trains were more than 20 minutes late just as often as they were on time. The early months of 1958 were particularly bad with trains showing up one and two hours late. From September 1958 onwards though, things suddenly improved, and W99 was thereafter on time at least half the time.

Of course, the mayhem may largely have been south of Crewe, as once the Blackpool portion was discarded, with a 7P or 8P on eight or nine coaches there should have been real potential for regaining time not just keeping it. There are a couple of instances in Alec's records showing that being done. Here's Paul Irving's interpretation of Alec's journey home from Crewe on W99 on Saturday, 14th June 1958:

It seems that 5-34 pm was the actual departure time, one hour late . . . Warrington was passed in an excellent time from Crewe at 5-57.30 — 24.2 miles in 23½ minutes. A TSR was encountered at Winwick Junction, but Wigan did well, reducing the station allowance from 6 to 2½ minutes, for a departure 54½ minutes late at 6-16½ pm. Preston did its bit as well; the train was there from 6-34½ pm to 6-38 pm, departing 45 minutes late.

An excellent run ensued on to Lancaster, 21 miles in 21 minutes 30 secs. start to stop. This saw W99 depart from Lancaster 43 minutes late at 7-02 pm. More smart station work took place at Carnforth, 7-12–7-14 pm and his train arrived in Oxenholme at 7-29 pm, 38 minutes late. This is a good illustration of all concerned, footplate crew, signalmen and station staff doing everything possible to get the train back to RT. With a schedule of 96 minutes between departure from Oxenholme and departing Carlisle (50 miles), my guess is that W99 went into the Scottish Region at or very near right time!

Upperby Rebuilt Scot 46141 *The North Staffordshire Regiment* accelerates the modest eight-coach load of W99 the 1-35 pm Euston–Perth north from Lancaster past Barley Cop Lane, a Blackpool portion having been detached at Crewe. Saturday, 20th April 1957. CRA Pearsall Collection PEJ766.

W484 c.12-20 pm Perth–Euston

W484, the 'afternoon' Perth–Euston left Perth typically at 12-20 pm and didn't arrive in Euston until around 10-00 pm. In the winter timetable period it comprised a modest seven coaches leaving Perth, and, in the late 1950s, it would add a few coaches at Carlisle making a ten- or eleven-coach train. On weekdays in Winter 1957/8 the portion added at Carlisle was actually four coaches that left Glasgow Central at 1-30 pm, the traditional departure time of the Up Midday Scot, but in that timetable the weekday Midday was leaving Glasgow at the unorthodox hour of 3-00 pm. On Saturdays the Midday ran at its normal 1-30 pm time and the coaches added at Carlisle started there. The following winter, the Midday reverted to its 1-30 pm departure time, and W484 added but a single coach Monday–Thursday at Carlisle, increased to three on Fridays and Saturdays.

In Summer 1957, W484 ran as nine coaches from Perth and four from Glasgow on weekdays, becoming ten plus two on Saturdays. But the following summer W484 was extended backwards to become the 10-20 am from Aberdeen. Running *via* Forfar between Aberdeen and Perth, it was typically a modest three (SX) or five (SO) coaches, but, with eight added at Perth, including a dining section, it became a fully-fledged 11- to 13- coach affair with nothing to be added at Carlisle.

In contrast to its northbound counterpart W99 though, W484 largely shunned Cumbrian travellers and didn't stop between leaving Carlisle just before 4-00 pm and reaching Lancaster around 5-15 pm. Nor were there Blackpool portions to be collected further south.

It seems W484 was generally scheduled to change engines at Carlisle; an Upperby loco and crew taking over to work through to Euston. Alec's records of W484, about two-thirds of which were on a Saturday, show that the train engine was invariably nothing less than a 7P, and from mid-1959 8Ps began to predominate. As if this weren't profligate enough, for a period through until September 1958 pilots were often provided, especially on summer Saturdays, and not just 2Ps but frequently 'Black Fives' or 6Ps. Perhaps the latter though, as Paul Irving suggests, was expediency rather than profligacy and just a convenient way of shifting surplus 5s and 6s back south, these typically being Crewe North or Camden locos?

In contrast to many other trains Alec recorded passing through Oxenholme, 'foreign' locos from depots other than Upperby and the latter two depots were conspicuous by their absence. Not one for the spotters this, only the very occasional Edge Hill or Longsight 7P. Alec first recorded a diesel on W484 on Monday, 1st August 1960, when it was Camden 'Peak' D2 *Helvellyn* doing the honours.

Timekeeping, again for a modestly-loaded, modestly-timed train, was pretty grim. Across around 90 observations over the years, fewer than one in three trains passed Oxenholme on time. Almost a quarter were more than 20 minutes late, and more than 40% of trains were more than ten minutes late. Once again, Summer 1958 was particularly gruesome with nearly half Alec's sightings more than 20 minutes late, and on average these were over 40 minutes late. In not a single season over four and a half years did W484 reach 40% right time or early.

Rebuilt Patriot No. 45512 *Bunsen*, an Upperby loco throughout the 1950s until late 1964, near the end of her days, hurries W484, the 12-20 pm Perth–Euston express through Deepthwaite cutting south of Hincaster Junction on Thursday, 10th April 1958. CRA Pearsall Collection PEK215.

Lancashire – Glasgow & Edinburgh

The service of trains connecting the Lancashire cities of Manchester and Liverpool with Glasgow and Edinburgh was among the most complex and the most variable with the seasons, high days and holidays, of all those passing through Oxenholme. At its simplest, on winter weekdays, the service comprised morning (C384 Down and W282 Up) and late afternoon trains (C402 Down and W140 Up) between the pairs of cities, portions typically being combined or split off at Preston and Carstairs. This was supplemented by a lunchtime Manchester–Carlisle (C400) that continued to Glasgow on Saturdays and W128, a tea-time Carlisle–Preston service, which was prone to being extended back to Glasgow and south to Liverpool/Manchester whenever things got busy. In summer, these multi-portion trains could run as two, three or even four separate trains, sometimes with extra portions for other destinations.

There isn't nearly enough space here to cover all their complexities, let alone the variations from year to year, but the morning trains will serve as examples to give a flavour of the goings on. The first train of the day was C384, and in Winter 1957/8, the first of Alec's records, this originated (according to the Passenger Train Marshalling book of the day) as the 9-30 am Manchester Victoria to Glasgow Central. Between Manchester and Preston it was a mere five coaches, but at Preston nine more were attached on the rear. These had set out as the 9-43 am from Liverpool Exchange and comprised a six-coach portion for Glasgow Central plus a further three coaches for Edinburgh Princes St, which would be detached at Carstairs. C384, now a heavy 14-coach train, ran non-stop from Preston to Carlisle and was timed to pass Oxenholme at 11-30 am.

In summer, and often also on busy weekends or holidays, this train became two trains, C384 from Manchester Victoria, and C386 from Liverpool Exchange that followed from Preston hard on its heels. In Summer 1957 for example, C384 again ran non-stop from Preston to Carlisle passing Oxenholme at 11-15 am while C386 called at Lancaster Castle and was due to pass just eleven minutes later. Each train comprised around a dozen coaches, and each had both Glasgow and Edinburgh portions, which were detached at Carstairs. Often, it seems, Edinburgh passengers on the Manchester train had to kick their heels for as much as ¾ of an hour waiting for the Liverpool coaches to arrive so they could proceed as a combined train to the Scottish capital. And on peak summer Saturdays, a third train was added to the morning service in the shape of C390, the 9-15 am Liverpool Exchange to Glasgow Central, which included a portion from Southport Chapel St.

The corresponding southbound service, W282, departed Glasgow Central on winter weekdays at 11-00 am as an eleven-coach train with the five coaches for Manchester Victoria leading and six for Liverpool Exchange behind. Three more coaches for Liverpool left Edinburgh at 11-05 am and were attached to the other Liverpool coaches at Carstairs. In contrast to the northbound morning service, W282 called at stations in Cumbria on its way south. In Winter 1956/7 for example, W282 called at Penrith, Oxenholme (2-43–2-47 pm) and then Carnforth and Lancaster.

In summer though, things changed; taking 1957 as an example, W282 became a Glasgow-only to Manchester train of just seven coaches and leaving Glasgow Central at 10-50 am it ran not *via* the direct route over Beattock but *via* the GSW line through Nithsdale and Dumfries. On weekdays it then ran non-stop from Carlisle to Lancaster. W282 was followed out of Glasgow Central five minutes later by W432, the 10-55 am to Liverpool Exchange, which by taking the usual Caledonian route arrived at Carlisle ahead of W282 even though it stopped at Carstairs to attach an Edinburgh portion. W432 also ran non-stop on summer weekdays from Carlisle to Preston.

On Saturdays in summer, the service was ramped up further. The 10-55 am to Liverpool became a Glasgow-only train and the Edinburgh portion became a separate train, W284, the 11-10 am Edinburgh Princes St – Liverpool Exchange, which just for good measure also had a Manchester portion. Are you following all this . . . ?!

W282 itself now acquired a five-coach portion for Morecambe, which was detached during an unadvertised stop at Carnforth. Sometimes, however, W282 ran as two separate trains, W282-1 and W282-2, only one of which had a Morecambe portion. So the single train of winter weekdays would often become four separate trains on summer Saturdays.

The Lancashire to Scotland services were very much the preserve of three sheds. Polmadie provided the lion's share of the locos from its complement of five 7P Rebuilt Scots (46102/4/5/7 and 21), five Britannias (70050-4) and its five 6P Clan 4-6-2s (72000-4). For the Manchester trains, C384 and W282, Newton Heath provided most of the balance from its fleet of 6P Jubilees, which in 1957 were 45635/42/61/700/1/2/6/10/12. Bank Hall's Jubilees 45698/717/9 *Mars, Dauntless* and *Glorious* appeared mainly in summer when the Liverpool portions became separate through trains.

Another source of fascination with the Lancashire to Scotland trains was the frequent double-heading, and for northbound trains there were spasmodic occasions when single-engined trains stopped 'out of course' at Oxenholme to attach a pilot for the climb through the Westmorland fells. This practice invariably involved the attachment of one of Oxenholme's 2-6-4Ts and was for some obscure reason known locally as 'putting a sock on it'. About 10% of the single-headed trains felt the need to stop for assistance and attach a 'sock'. As would be expected, 6P Jubilees and Clans called for a 'sock' more often *pro rata* than did the 7P Scots and Britannias.

Alec recorded the passage of C384 some 222 times, 90% of his sightings being on weekdays, and the motive power provision changed markedly across the years and seasons. In Summer 1957, when C384 was an eleven-coach train with C386 running separately from Liverpool, it appeared over 80% of the time entrusted to a solo 6P, normally a Newton Heath Jubilee, with just a couple of appearances from a Polmadie Clan; a 7P or a pilot was provided on only a couple of his dozen sightings. During Winter 1957/8, when running as a combined 14-coach train, the loco was unsurprisingly most often a solo Polmadie 7P Rebuilt Scot or Britannia, and even on the 25% of occasions when a pilot was provided the train engine was still a 7P more often than not. A solo 6P appeared only on a couple of occasions, and stopped for a banker on one of those.

Come Summer 1958 and the 6Ps were back as train engine most of the time, assisted by a pilot on half the trains and only in sole charge on a third of them. Then in September 1958 it was back to Polmadie 7Ps, which were in sole charge of around three-quarters of Alec's 70-odd sightings, while a 6P had sole charge only once. A pilot was provided for 20% of trains during Winter 1958/9, with 6Ps and 7Ps sharing equally the duty as train engine. Summer 1959 saw 6Ps back almost as often as the previous year, but after that they faded from the picture and by Summer 1960 7Ps were in sole charge of almost 90% of trains, with pilot provision almost eliminated. While piloting from the south steadily became less common however, an increasing number of trains stopped out of course at Oxenholme for assistance from a 2-6-4T 'sock' – some 13% in Winter 1959/60 and 18% in Winter 1960/61. Over the years, while 6Ps stopped for help more often than 7Ps, on 40% of occasions they tackled the climb into the fells unaided.

Polmadie's five Clan Pacifics were regular performers on the Lancashire–Scotland services. On Saturday, 22nd June 1957 72004 *Clan Macdonald* approaches Castle station right on time on the dot of 6 pm and crosses to the Up platform line with Up express passenger W128. In winter, W128 was the lowly 4-10 pm Carlisle–Preston but on such summer Saturdays W128 blossomed into the 1-45 pm Glasgow Central (and Edinburgh) to Liverpool Exchange and Manchester Victoria. CRA Mayor Collection MAY085.

Polmadie Scot 46107 *Argyll & Sutherland Highlander* crosses Docker Viaduct in fine style with a Down express and attacks the final two miles to Grayrigg as the gradient stiffens to 1 in 106. Alec's notebooks suggest this is Thursday, 30th April 1959 and 46107 is running right time on C384, the 9-30 am Manchester Victoria–Glasgow Central. CRA Mayor Collection MAY298.

LMS 2P 4-4-0s from Upperby or Preston were frequent pilots on Scotland–Lancashire trains until the late 1950s. Preston 2P 40694 pilots Polmadie Britannia 70054 *Dornoch Firth* on a Glasgow–Manchester express near Yealand on Saturday, 20th April 1957. Despite the mighty appearance of the Britannia with its high-sided BR1D tender, they were only two-cylinder 7Ps, and with 16 coaches in tow the pilot's assistance was probably much appreciated. CRA Pearsall Collection PEJ763.

There were also changing patterns in the locos provided as pilots from the south too. In the first twelve months of Alec's observations, until mid-1958, the pilots were generally LMS 2P 4-4-0s belonging to Upperby, or sometimes Preston, though the last 2P pilot Alec noted on C384, on Friday, 5th June 1959, was 40588 of Bank Hall MPD assisting Polmadie's 70050 *Firth of Clyde*. From mid-1958, 'Black Fives' became the most common pilot provided, and while these were often still Preston or Upperby locos, it was equally likely to be one from another shed on the West Coast main line, ranging from Aston, Crewe North and South, Warrington and Newton Heath in the south to Kingmoor, Motherwell and Polmadie. On four occasions 'Black Fives' were used as the train engine, but only when in tandem with another of the class. Occasionally, C384 appeared with super-power, having a 6P Patriot or Jubilee as pilot, in tandem with another 6P. On Friday 22nd May 1959 there was a full '13P' on the front with Patriot 45542 assisting Polmadie Britannia 70050 *Firth of Clyde*.

It's at first perhaps surprising that given the climb from Carlisle to Shap is less arduous than that from Oxenholme, a greater proportion of the southbound W282 morning Glasgow–Manchester trains had a pilot than did the northbound C384. Paul Irving again comments, however, that in many cases the pilot was attached more as a positioning move to get a southern-based loco back south than for the assistance it provided. That said, W282's train engine was a 6P or even a 'Black Five', as opposed to a 7P, on more than 35% of occasions compared to less than 25% for the northbound C384. All the 'Black Fives' took a pilot, but otherwise 7Ps were just as likely to be given a pilot as 6Ps. That does suggest operating convenience was an important factor.

Looking at the pilots themselves, of the 55 recorded by Alec some 18 were 2Ps, the last of these being sighted in January 1959. Most of these were Upperby or Preston locos for which piloting would be their *raison d'etre* on these trains, as it would too for 42664, an Upperby 2-6-4T that once appeared. Most of the remainder were 5MTs (28 'Black Fives' plus Stanier Mogul 42966), though seven 6Ps were used (Jubilees plus one Patriot 45511 *Isle of Man*). Of these 36 larger locos, just ten were Carlisle engines (seven Upperby and three Kingmoor), which would also logically be attached for the purpose of assistance. The remainder, around half the pilots used, were large locos from sheds south of Cumbria (Crewe North and South, Aston and Edge Hill accounting for most) where repatriation may have been at least a convenient outcome if not the main reason for their attachment in the first place.

The timekeeping of the morning Manchester–Glasgow varied over the years and seasons too – from consistently good to frequently awful. Over the period of Alec's records, C384 passed through Oxenholme right time or early almost half the time. A quarter of the trains were more than five minutes late with 6% being more than 20 minutes late. Timekeeping in Summer 1957 with Newton Heath Jubilees mostly in sole charge was good, 75% of the trains Alec recorded being right time or early. In Winter 1957/8, with heavier trains but 7Ps up front, this figure was down to 47%.

Strangely, in Summer 1958 when many trains were piloted, 80% were more than five minutes late and a couple were over an hour late, both incidentally on weekdays. Overall, the timekeeping was best with a solo 7P on the front, with only 10% of trains more than five minutes late. The peak was reached in Summer 1960 with 7Ps in charge of nearly 90% of trains and over 80% were right time or early. Piloted trains were late more often, as were the solo 6Ps, but inevitably worst of all were the occasions when trains stopped out of course at Oxenholme to attach a 2-6-4T 'sock', two-thirds being at least ten minutes late.

The timekeeping of the southbound morning service W282 over the years that Alec observed it was overall significantly worse than for example W126, the Up Midday Scot, which similarly travelled from Glasgow. This wasn't so much in terms of how often the trains appeared at Oxenholme on time (both around a third of occasions) but the degree of lateness. While W126 was more than ten minutes late around 25% of the time, and more than 20 minutes late on about 10% of runs, W282 was more than ten minutes late on 40% of Alec's sightings and more than 20 minutes late more than 25% of the time.

During 1958, 'Black Fives' became regular pilots for Scotland–Lancashire services in place of ageing 2P 4-4-0s. Crewe North 'Black Five' 44763 as pilot and Polmadie Rebuilt Scot 4-6-0 46107 *Argyll and Sutherland Highlander* restart W282, the 11-00 am Glasgow Central to Manchester Victoria, from its Oxenholme stop on Saturday, 15th March 1958. CRA Mayor Collection MAY350.

Analysing Alec's records, another thing stands out — W282's timekeeping was much worse during the summer timetable period. During the winter timetable periods from 1957 through to 1960, W282 made a right time or better arrival at Oxenholme on almost half the occasions, and was more than 20 minutes late less than 20% of the time. But in summer it was just the opposite. It passed through right time or early less than 20% of the time and more than half the time it was over 20 minutes late — and when it was late, it was very, very late. For example, in Summer 1958, which seems to have been something of an *'annus horribilis'* for W282, its lateness when over 20 minutes late actually averaged no less than 50 minutes late!

The explanation as to why this should be so, however, is doubtless very complex. While W282 could be a very different train at different times of the year, on Saturdays when more than three quarters of Alec's observations were made, it was an eleven-coach train both winter and summer. During the winter timetable period it combined portions from Glasgow and Edinburgh to Manchester and Liverpool, whereas on summer Saturdays it combined just a Manchester and Morecambe portion, though it ran *via* the GSWR route to Carlisle.

The winter and summer schedules in 1957/8 were also very similar, the summer train being allowed 74 minutes from departing Carlisle to passing Oxenholme, before stopping at Carnforth to detach the Morecambe portion. The winter train stopped at Penrith for six minutes and again at Oxenholme, so the allowance of 83 minutes including the Penrith stop looks no easier at all. Was the summer routing *via* the GSW perhaps a factor? In the absence of time keeping data at Carlisle that's hard to say.

It's even difficult to put it all down simply to summer Saturday congestion: the Up Midday Scot for example in Summer 1958 did run late more often on Saturdays, but was more than 20 minutes late only one third of the time compared to two-thirds for W282. Maybe of course the Midday Scot was higher up the pecking order, and was shepherded through by the train controllers? Or maybe 1 pm when W282 was nearing Carlisle was a much worse time to be doing that than when the Midday approached two hours later? Interesting, but inconclusive!

Windermere expresses

Windermere and Kendal were served by four Up and four Down expresses that linked the southern Lakes year round variously to London, Crewe, Manchester and Preston. In summer of course these services were substantially augmented with expresses also to/from Liverpool and Blackpool as well as seasonal extras. Alec's observations were inevitably more numerous for the year-round daytime trains.

A Britannia Pacific, doubtless one of the Polmadie 'Firths', with 13 or 14 coaches in tow thunders north towards Oxenholme station past the MPD with a morning Lancashire–Scotland express, probably in the mid-1950s. CRA Mayor Collection MAY267.

W204 8-10 am Windermere–Manchester

The first train regularly noted by Alec was one it seems he saw almost daily, possibly from his breakfast table. This was W204, typically departing Windermere at 8-10 am for Manchester Exchange, and the successor to the 'Club' train that was introduced in 1905 by the LNWR to convey Manchester businessmen to and from their Lake District homes in style. On weekdays in Alec's time it was a train of eight or nine coaches, the rear two of which were through-coaches for Liverpool Exchange which were transferred at Preston to a Blackpool–Liverpool express. The Manchester portion included a First Open, a more prosaic but still comfortable version of the erstwhile Club Car. On Saturdays there was neither a First Open nor a Liverpool portion.

Alec's 635 sightings of W204 show the loco was routinely provided by Crewe North MPD. Just over half the time this was a 7P, most often a Rebuilt Scot, but Rebuilt Patriots and Jubilees, and Britannias also featured. The rest of the time it was usually a 6P, generally a Jubilee, but unrebuilt Patriots occasionally appeared too. On 10% of occasions though the job was entrusted to a 'Black Five'.

The loco arrived in Windermere earlier the same morning on the 'Mail', which started out around 11-00 pm from Euston as a train of around twelve coaches, most of which ended up in Blackpool or Whitehaven, leaving only a Corridor Brake Composite (BCK) and a BG to run through to Windermere. Alec noted five occasions when W204 appeared behind an Oxenholme 2-6-4T, indicating some major delay or mishap to the 'Mail' en route from London.

Three times out of four, the loco provided for W204 was one of Crewe North's own, and although nearly 80 different 5A-allocated 6Ps and 7Ps were used over the four years from 1958 through 1961, just six of them — Rebuilt Patriot 45529 *Stephenson*, Jubilees 45625 *Sarawak*, 45684 *Jutland* and 45726 *Vindictive*, Rebuilt Jubilee 45736 *Phoenix*

The sun is still well in the east on a summer morning between 1957 and 1959 as Crewe North Jubilee 4-6-0 45586 *Mysore* approaches Kendal station from Windermere with what must surely be W204, the 8-10 am Windermere–Manchester 'Club' train. Some of Kendal's sizeable goods yard is visible on the left. CRA Mayor Collection MAY048.

and Rebuilt Scot 46128 *The Lovat Scouts* — handled around 80 of the trains between them.

Over 160 of the locos provided by Crewe North, however, were 'foreign' locos belonging to other sheds. The diagram that included W204 was known to be frequently used for 'running-in' locos overhauled at Crewe Works, and comparing Alec's sightings of 'foreign' engines against dates officially on Works as noted on each engine's Record Card reveals that over a hundred of them had been released from Works during the previous week or two. It seems two or three locos were actually sent out to work W204 *before* being handed over to the Works, and a couple appeared in the middle of an especially long spell on Works, perhaps indicating a problem that took a long time to resolve.

So, for the early-bird spotter on the Windermere branch, the morning 'Club' train offered the prospect of something really juicy from time to time. Jubilees from the Midland Division and Bushbury would normally be rare birds in Cumbria, but Kentish Town's 45561 *Saskatchewan*, 45575 *Madras*, 45585 *Hyderabad* and 45622 *Nyasaland,* Derby's 45626 *Seychelles*, Nottingham's 45641 *Sandwich* and 45650 *Blake*, Millhouses' 45654 *Hood* and Bristol Barrow Road's 45651 *Shovell* all put in appearances on W204 after release from Works. So too did 45734 *Meteor* and 45742 *Connaught,* Bushbury locos that normally spent their time on Wolverhampton–London expresses.

The other 60 or so 'foreign' locos that turned up on the morning 'Club' train were from some 20 different sheds, mostly on the Western Division of the LM Region, including a good number from Preston, Carnforth and Upperby. Many were doubtless conveniently appropriated while passing through when 5A was short of power for some reason or, in the case of wandering Scottish and Upperby locos, perhaps a first step towards easing them back north.

W55 5-10 pm SX Manchester Exchange –Windermere and W370 8-30 pm Windermere–Euston

As far as the stock and the businessmen who travelled in it were concerned, the return working of W204 was W55, the 5-10 pm SX Manchester Exchange–Windermere, which collected the two-coach Liverpool portion again at Preston (on Saturdays the stock of W204 was despatched as a lunchtime train to Llandudno and re-appeared in Windermere *via* Preston in the early hours of Monday morning). The loco that took W204 to Manchester in the morning didn't bring it back though; that left Manchester with W37, the 3-54 pm to Barrow, as part of one of the famous LMS cyclic diagrams.

The loco that brought the 'Club' train back from Manchester in the evening, called at Oxenholme just after 7 pm and arrived in Windermere about 7-35 pm. It was quickly turned in order to take W370, the 8-30 pm Windermere–Euston back south, re-appearing at Oxenholme about 9 pm. Alec was rarely around to record W55, having his evening meal perhaps, but more frequently saw W370 as he was wont to return to Oxenholme station to see the Down Caledonian go north about ten past eight.

Taking Alec's observations of the two trains together, it's clear that these were in a Crewe North loco diagram too, as 44 of the 59 sightings were 5A locos and six of the 15 'foreign' locos had been in Works within the last week or two. Jubilees predominated, and 'Black Fives' appeared on about a quarter of the trains, with only a few Scots or unrebuilt Patriots involved. The remaining nine 'foreign' locos would have provided no little interest for local enthusiasts though, as in addition to the odd Preston and Upperby locos, Windermere was visited by an Aston 'Black Five', two Holyhead Standard 5MTs,

The Windermere 'Club' train is seen returning from Manchester as W55, the 5-10 pm Manchester–Windermere. Unrebuilt Patriot 4-6-0 45503 *The Royal Leicestershire Regiment* of Crewe North climbs the 1 in 134 near Yealand, north of Carnforth, with a substantial rake of nine coaches on Friday, 26th June 1959. CRA Pearsall Collection PEK674.

A 'foreigner' on the 'Club' train. From w/e 23rd July 1962, former Millhouses Jubilee 45683 *Hogue*, which had been placed into store at Staveley GC MPD when Millhouses closed at the end of 1961, was re-allocated to Sheffield Darnall for use on summer extra services. Somehow, 45683, complete with 41A Darnall shedplate, has found her way onto W55, the returning 'Club' train, and stands in the 'Bay' platform at Oxenholme ready for the last leg to Windermere, probably in July 1962. CRA Irvine Collection IRV019.

a Farnley Junction Jubilee and, most exotic of all, 45396 of Stirling and Caprotti Standard 5MT 73124 of Corkerhill.

Paul Irving comments throughout the period of Alec's notes that the loco hauling W370 probably took the train only as far as Preston where a Camden Rebuilt Scot was booked to take over. For while the train left Windermere as a mere six coaches, taking the Winter of 1957/8 as an example, even by the time it left Lancaster it sometimes would have acquired another ten. First, W370 combined at Carnforth with W256, the 6-27 pm from Workington, whose six coaches, or seven on a Friday, were shunted onto the front. At the head of W256 was a Mail section comprising a Post Office Sorting Coach and two BGs, followed by three or four passenger coaches. Then at Lancaster, three sleeping cars from Barrow were attached to the rear, having arrived on the 5-08 pm from Workington. This was already some 15 or 16 coaches weighing around 500 tons: some load if the Jubilee, or even 'Black Five', was supposed to get it to Preston! At Preston, the load was marginally eased, as the PO vehicle and leading BG were detached while another heavy sleeping car was added to the rear. Finally, at Crewe, another BG was added off the 11-30 pm newspaper train from Manchester London Road and departing at 12-25 am W370 then ran non-stop to arrive in Euston at the unearthly hour of 3-39 am.

By 1962, the working of W55 and W370 had become part of a four-day cyclic diagram for a Carnforth Patriot, which had wandered up and down the West Coast main line between Crewe, Barrow and Morecambe/Heysham for three days before arriving in Manchester with the 7-00 am express from Barrow. Now, the loco went no further south with W370 than Carnforth.

On Saturdays, W370 was a more modest affair beyond Carnforth. It still left Windermere as six coaches, now behind an Oxenholme 2-6-4T, as W55 did not run on Saturdays. But there was no PO Sorting Coach from Workington, nor did the sleepers run from Barrow, so the train stayed at eleven coaches all the way to Euston, swapping only a BG for a sleeping car at Preston.

The process for assembling the Up Lakes Express at Oxenholme is neatly illustrated in this photo taken from the Workington portion, standing in the Up Main platform. The Fowler 2-6-4T, which has brought this in from Penrith, has detached and stands in the Down Main platform ready to go to the MPD. Meanwhile, the Jubilee which brought the Windermere portion moves it out of the 'Bay' prior to reversing onto the Workington portion, coupling up, and departing south. Saturday, 16th June 1956. Image by kind permission of Ernie's Railway Archive.

W86 c.11-00 am Windermere–Crewe / Euston (and Up Lakes Express)

The main express of the day from Windermere to the South was W86, which consistently departed around the agreeable hour of 11 am, but whose make-up leaving Oxenholme ranged from four coaches on winter weekdays to a full 15 coaches in high summer. In the winter timetable period it ran only as far as Crewe during the week, and it was no more than a four-coach train until it reached Preston where it attached a further four coaches from Blackpool. On Fridays and Saturdays however, W86 ran through to Euston. It was half as long again on Fridays, with both Windermere and Blackpool portions now comprising six coaches, while on Saturdays it left Windermere as a full eight-coach train and ran as such right through to London.

Come summer though, things changed. Taking the Summer Timetable of 1959 as an example, outside the high season from July to early September, W86 still ran to Crewe and in much the same form during the week. On Fridays six coaches from Windermere were joined by a further five from Blackpool to run through to Euston. Departure time from Monday to Friday was now 11-10 am, and from Tuesday to Friday two BGs from Heysham were collected at Preston and taken to Crewe. On Saturdays though, departure time was brought forward to 10-50 am, and still outside the peak season a reduced complement of five coaches from Windermere was now joined at Oxenholme by a seven-coach portion from Workington, which ran *via* Keswick and Penrith. A dining section comprising a Restaurant First and a Second Open was attached at Preston.

During the peak holiday weeks each summer, which in 1959 ran from 6th July to 5th September, W86 became the titled Lakes Express. Now there was a five-coach Workington portion to be attached at Oxenholme and the train ran through to Euston every day from Monday to Saturday. On weekdays the train left Windermere with seven coaches, the Restaurant First now being part of the starting rake, but two of the Workington coaches were detached at Lancaster.

The Blackpool portion added in various forms at Preston took the train up to as many as 16 coaches. On Saturdays during these peak weeks, the Windermere portion was again eight coaches and the Workington portion, with three from Workington plus four from Keswick, took the Lakes Express to a full 15 coaches leaving Oxenholme.

Of course, these timetabled patterns of working were subject to adjustment in Special Traffic Notices, so at busy times pre- and post-holidays for example, W86 would get extended to Euston as required.

Being barely ten miles from its starting point, the punctuality of arrival of W86 at Oxenholme wasn't likely to be remarked on. But Alec often noted that, especially in winter when the timings were closer, if the Up Caledonian was running late, the departure of W86 was invariably delayed. With stops at Carnforth, Lancaster and Preston, W86 wasn't going to be put ahead of a late-running crack express!

In the winter months, with no portion from Workington and Keswick to be attached, W86, the 11-00 am express from Windermere, departed south directly from the 'Bay', heading for Crewe during the week but often through to Euston on Fridays and Saturdays. W86 is seen departing in the winter or early spring of 1951/2 behind Jubilee 45673 *Keppel,* which was a Preston loco until September 1952 when she moved north becoming a Scottish Region engine for the rest of her days.
CRA Mayor Collection MAY141.

Alec's 200 sightings of W86 show it was hauled from Windermere on more than 90% of occasions either by 6Ps (Jubilees or Patriots), or just 'Black Fives', with equal frequency. The loco seems normally to have arrived both winter and summer on W279, the *circa* 8-15 am Preston–Windermere, though Alec's records are essentially empty of sightings of W279, which passed through Oxenholme just after 9-30 am each morning when he was probably at his desk at the *Gazette*.

Alec rarely recorded a 7P on W86 until 1960, by which time Preston MPD had acquired about ten Scots. That said, very few of Alec's sightings were on summer Saturdays when the train was at its heaviest leaving Oxenholme, but during the peak weeks when every day W86 became The Lakes Express, with twelve coaches to Lancaster and ten thence to Preston, the loco was more often a 5MT than anything else. Records assembled by Chris Coates's 'West Coast Sightings Sheets' group show that by 1960 Scots were the usual power on summer Saturdays, with an engine change frequently to another Scot at Preston for the rest of the trip to Euston. Paul Irving suggests that when W86 ran through to Euston, the engine was probably changed at Preston for a Camden 7P.

It appears that Preston generally provided the loco for W86 during the winter timetable period while Upperby provided it in summer, though an exception was the first half of 1959 when it seems Upperby regularly covered the duty. During the second half of 1961, Preston and Upperby then disappeared from the picture and it became Crewe North or Camden locos that Alec would see on W86.

Looking more closely at the 35 occasions when 'foreign' locos turned up on W86, some interesting patterns emerge, especially as regards Mondays! Of Alec's 33 sightings of W86 on a Monday before Summer 1960, when things seemed to settle, only a dozen were Preston or Upperby locos and fewer still conformed to the winter/summer pattern just noted. The rest came from a whole variety of Western and Central Division sheds; a couple were recently released from Crewe Works, and seven came from Kingmoor or Scotland. Checking back into Alec's records reveals that six of these seven, which all appeared in summer, had the previous Saturday piloted an express from Scotland to Liverpool, or in one case Manchester. So was the subsequent use on W86, heading south of course, a constructive step towards repatriation, or just an opportunistic purloining of a spare loco? 'Black Five' 45086 of Dalry Road even managed to do the circuit twice in successive weeks in August 1959!

W33 6-40 am Euston–Windermere

If W86, leaving Windermere at 11-00 am, offered the most civilised way to travel to London, then W33, the only year-round northbound daytime counterpart certainly wasn't the civilised way to come back. Not only did W33 leave Euston at the unwontedly early hour of 6-40 am, it took the best part of eight hours to complete the journey, wandering north by way of Northampton, dropping BGs loaded with parcels at various points, and not arriving in Windermere until well into the afternoon.

For most of the year, W33 appeared at Oxenholme soon after 2 pm as a prosaic five- or six-coach train, having shed a Barrow and Workington portion at Lancaster. But on peak summer Saturdays, Oxenholme was treated to a unique event when a four-coach portion arrived from Leeds, *via* Arnside and Hincaster Junction, and was attached to the rear of W33 for the final leg of the journey to Windermere.

During the week, the loco that brought in W33 was turned at Windermere and returned light engine as far as Kendal where it then took charge of the often heavy 6-35 pm parcels from Kendal to London. On Saturdays, the loco would typically return LE to Carnforth.

Most of Alec Mayor's observations of W33 at Oxenholme were on Saturdays, and in a good number of cases he was only there later in the afternoon to see the returning light engine, not W33 itself. Surprisingly, there are no records in Paul Irving's compiled notebooks of the locos that brought in the summer Saturday Leeds portion, but it's believed these were

By the early 1960s, W33 reached Oxenholme as an even more modest train of two or three coaches plus a BG. Being a Saturday, 24th September 1960, Longsight Caprotti 'Black Five' 44748 has the extra SK that often ran MFSO behind the tender as she climbs towards Hincaster Junction around 2 pm, over seven hours after leaving Euston. CRA Pearsall Collection A6032-5.

invariably 2-6-4Ts and maybe just reflects Alec's relative lack of interest in local passenger traffic.

There's a clear contrast between winter and summer timetables though in Alec's sightings of W33 or its engine. Most of the locos involved (around 80%) were 'Black Fives', with the odd Standard Class 5. The rest were 6Ps with just a couple of 7Ps. In the winter period the loco was normally provided by Upperby, at least until May 1959. After that date, and in the summer timetable periods, things seemed rather more haphazard. As was often the case, Preston and Crewe North locos were the most frequent after Upperby, but locos from a dozen different sheds scattered as far as Mold Junction, Patricroft and Fleetwood appeared on odd occasions.

Timekeeping too showed a stark contrast. In the winter timetable periods, Alec recorded only a single train that wasn't right time or early, and that was only a minute late! But in summer, perhaps unsurprisingly with most observations being on Saturdays, more than half were over 20 minutes late, and averaged 30 late.

W121 Down Lakes Express

The best way to travel from London to Windermere was surely on W121, though this only ran in summer. In the peak weeks, this was famous as The Lakes Express. In 1957, for example, W121 began running on Saturdays at the start of the summer timetable period in June, leaving Euston as the 11-52 am to Workington. Then from the 8th July it began running on weekdays as well, and, taking the title of The Lakes Express, continued six days a week until the 7th September, the penultimate Saturday of the timetable period.

W121 left Euston as a 14-coach train and during the week it was made up of three portions. At the front was a three-coach portion for Workington *via* Keswick; next was a six-coach portion for Windermere including a dining section and at the rear was a five-coach portion for Barrow and Whitehaven. The latter portion was transferred at Crewe to the 3-05 pm Crewe–Workington, so the Lakes Express went forward to Oxenholme as a nine-coach train. On Saturdays, however, W121's 14 coaches comprised just two portions, the Workington via Keswick portion now being five coaches and the Windermere portion now had nine. The Barrow and Workington portion became a separate train departing at 12 noon and including a portion for Morecambe.

Arriving at Oxenholme at 5-22 pm, W121 pulled into the Down Main platform. Five minutes later the train engine took the Workington portion off to Penrith where it ran into the Keswick back platform, before uncoupling and drifting off light engine to Upperby MPD. A fresh engine, typically an Ivatt 2MT 2-6-0, coupled onto the rear at Penrith and set off in the reverse direction for Keswick and Workington, running now, despite the Lakes Express carriage boards it would be carrying, as a Class B train. Meanwhile, the Windermere portion would be taken forward from Oxenholme at 5-35 pm by a locally-allocated 2-6-4T, also running now as a Class B and stopping at every station along the branch before reaching Windermere at 6-05 pm.

Alec recorded W121 on some 30 occasions, mostly Saturdays. Most often the loco was a 7P, a Rebuilt Scot, Patriot or Jubilee, with a couple of appearances by Britannias. From Summer 1960, it was most often a Duchess, and once a Princess Royal, while on half a dozen occasions across the years a 'Black Five' had to suffice.

Somewhat unusually, Edge Hill locos were frequent performers on W121, and together with Crewe North covered most of the Saturday duties in the Summers of 1958 and 1959, Upperby Duchesses then becoming the usual fare. The remaining occasions, mostly weekdays, were covered by locos from seven different sheds, including a few Scottish strays such as 45086 of Dalry Road that spent over a week south of the border and featured also on the Up Lakes on two successive Mondays in August 1959.

Alec's observations of W121 once again show timekeeping on summer Saturdays in 1958 to have been markedly poorer than the following summer. In 1958, W121 turned up on time on less than 25% of occasions, otherwise averaging around 20 minutes late. In 1959, however, W121 was on time or early more often than not.

Carlisle expresses

W74 c.8-30 am Carlisle–Euston

Train W74, the morning Carlisle and Windermere to London Euston passenger service, was by any standards a heavy train, routinely comprising 16 vehicles from Lancaster southwards. In BR days, it ran daily, including Saturdays and over the whole of that period the main train from Carlisle had a scheduled departure time around 8-30 am — 5–10 minutes earlier in some years and latterly up to ten minutes later.

W74 gathered its travellers from all over Cumberland and Westmorland, stopping at each place of importance on the main line

Holyhead Britannia Pacific 70048, named *The Territorial Army 1908-1958* barely a month earlier, re-starts the five-coach Workington portion of W121, the Down Lakes Express, up the gradient towards Grayrigg on Saturday, 30th August 1958. Having arrived right time at 5-22 pm, the Windermere portion of maybe nine coaches remains in the platform. CRA Mayor Collection MAY158.

south, as well as some rather less so, until it reached Crewe. Although it then stopped only twice before Euston, it took most of the day to get there, not arriving until teatime. So through passengers for London starting or connecting at Carlisle would be better advised to have the morning to themselves and take the Royal Scot at noon, which arrived in London barely an hour later.

But with stops at Preston, Wigan, Warrington and Crewe, W74 provided important connections for Cumbrians to most of the south and west of England, and Wales. W74 was also important for carrying Northern Irish parcels traffic south. Full Brakes were attached en route from Heysham, and in some years from Stranraer too, and ferried variously to Crewe, for Birmingham, and to London.

Taking the Winter of 1955/6 as an example, W74 started out from Carlisle as a nine-coach formation. On the front of the coaches was a Full Brake that, except for Mondays, came through to Carlisle along the Port Road from Stranraer on the 12-25 am (MX) parcels from there, and travelled daily all the way to Euston.

At Oxenholme, W74 collected a five-coach portion from Windermere, leaving there at 9-25 am, normally behind one of Oxenholme's 2-6-4Ts, and calling at all stations on the branch, Staveley, Burneside and Kendal. On arrival at Oxenholme, at 9-51 am in Winter 1955, the 2-6-4T would leave the Windermere coaches in the branch platform, referred to locally as the 'Bay', for W74's train engine to collect, during the nine-minute stop that followed its arrival at 9-58 am. It seems the procedure was for W74's loco to uncouple from its passenger coaches, retaining the Stranraer Brake, run forward on the Up Main, and reverse across the Down into the 'Bay'. The Windermere coaches were then drawn forward, reversed onto the Carlisle coaches in the Up platform, and W74 was re-coupled as a now substantial 14-coach rake, though it would be one coach lighter on Mondays.

At Lancaster, except on Mondays, two more Full Brakes were attached to the rear. These came from Heysham, brought by the 9-15 am parcels train from there to be ferried south to Crewe. This made the load up to a hefty 16 coaches in Winter 1955, and W74 became one of the heaviest of all passenger trains on the West Coast main line.

It's somewhat surprising then that in early 1958, until the introduction of the summer timetable in June, W74 was routinely hauled by a 7P 4-6-0. Even though the Carlisle and Windermere portions were each now one coach lighter than in 1955, lifting 14 coaches up the bank after the stop at Lancaster would still be a real challenge. Of the 22 occasions recorded by Alec Mayor at Oxenholme, an ex-LMS 7P 4-6-0 in the form of a Rebuilt Scot, Patriot or Jubilee was the motive power on all bar two occasions. The exceptions were Monday, 3rd February, when Upperby turned out one of its 6P Jubilees, 45588 *Kashmir*, and Thursday, 29th May when a Polmadie Britannia, 70053 *Moray Firth*, was given the job. On two occasions, the

Camden Coronation 4-6-2 46245 *City of London* climbs away from the future site of Hardendale quarry towards the Orton Road bridge on the last mile of the climb to Shap Summit with W74, the 8-30 am Carlisle–Euston express passenger, on Wednesday, 21st August 1957. With a load of some ten coaches already, the leading BG having come through from Stranraer, a further six from Windermere are likely to be added at Oxenholme, hence the 8P!
CRA Leslie Collection LES0476. By kind permission of Peter J Robinson.

LMS 7P was given a pilot — LMS 2P 4-4-0 40565 of Preston on Friday, 25th April, and super-power on Wednesday, 4th June when Jubilee 45553 *Canada* was on the front.

Mostly, the 7P train engine came from Crewe North MPD. A Camden 7P was noted on four occasions and an Upperby 7P twice. Just once, an Edge Hill 7P, Rebuilt Scot 46164 *The Artists' Rifleman* turned up, with the Preston 2P as a pilot.

At the start of the summer timetable on Monday, 9th June 1958, things changed. Carlisle Upperby was allocated six additional Duchesses, and they soon started making an appearance on the heavy W74, which had reverted to a 14-coach load from Oxenholme, indeed 15 on Fridays. Of nine occasions recorded by Alec Mayor before 14th September, when the summer timetable ended, a Duchess was on the front on seven of them, six being one of the Upperby locos, with Polmadie Pacific 46231 *Duchess of Atholl* appearing on the last Friday, 12th September.

In 1959, until the Autumn, both 7Ps and 8Ps from Crewe, Camden and Upperby were recorded pulling W74. Then things changed again, and on Monday, October 12th diesel power appeared in the form of EE Type 4 (latterly Class 40) D226. Through until the end of Alec Mayor's records in December 1961 diesels predominated on W74, but by no means monopolised it, as a third of Alec's sightings continued to be steam locos split evenly between Duchesses and 7Ps, though with one remarkable appearance on Friday, 30th June 1961 of a Preston 'Black Five', No. 45414, hauling this heavy train. The diesels were invariably EE Type 4s, though on Monday, 28th August 1961, 'Peak' D4 *Great Gable* was assigned the job.

Alec rarely recorded W74's timekeeping, doubtless as it was pretty regularly on time at Oxenholme having started only at Carlisle. He did, however, travel south on W74 from Preston to Wigan on a day of heavy snow, 25th February 1958, arriving there more than four hours late before calling it a day and heading home, as it happens on the corresponding northbound Euston to Carlisle train, W251!

W251 10-40 am Euston–Carlisle

Whereas W74 gathered portions as it journeyed south, W251 scattered them as it returned north. In Winter 1957/8 the starting load from Euston was 14 carriages, which were toted all the way to Lancaster. Here, on weekdays, a four-coach portion was detached to go forward to Barrow at 4-08 pm. On arrival at Oxenholme the front seven coaches, which contained the dining section RF + SO, were detached and taken on by the train engine to Carlisle leaving three to head down the branch as the 4-39 pm to Windermere. On Saturdays the formation was rather different in that the dining section was marshalled on the rear as part of the Barrow portion leaving just four coaches plus a BG completing the journey to Carlisle.

In Summer 1957 the formation was initially similar on weekdays, though with one coach more for Windermere and one less for Barrow. But during the peak weeks when W121, the Lakes Express, started running on weekdays to cater for Windermere passengers, the front nine coaches of W251 ran to Carlisle leaving just three for Barrow, except on Fridays when the Barrow portion was made up

A Duchess Pacific, probably Upperby's 46238 *City of Carlisle* heads W251 the 10-40 am Euston–Carlisle north near Holme, between Milnthorpe and Carnforth, around 4-15 pm if on time, on Wednesday, 13th April 1955.
CRA Pearsall Collection PEG366.

Oxenholme Fowler 2-6-4T 42313, carrying Class B lamps, departs from the Down Main platform onto the branch for Windermere with four corridor coaches. The London–Windermere carriage boards and the angle of the sun mark this out as the Windermere portion of W251, the 10-40 am Euston–Carlisle, detached from the main train and heading off for Windermere typically at 4-39 pm.
CRA Mayor Collection MAY153.

to six coaches. This same 15-coach formation applied on Saturdays throughout the timetable period, since W121 ran throughout on Saturdays, titled or not.

As for the motive power provided for this heavy train, well over half Alec's 170 or so sightings before EE Type 4s started to appear were Pacifics, almost all Duchesses. Barring a couple of occasions when W251 arrived double-headed by two 'Black Fives', or a 'Black Five' and a 6P Jubilee, the rest were rebuilt 7Ps — Scots, Patriots or Jubilees. All that is except for the 9th July 1958 when Upperby's 6P Patriot 45506 *The Royal Pioneer Corps* raised eyebrows by rolling W251 into Oxenholme right on time. Paul Irving commented that perhaps 45506 had taken over part way, or perhaps dispensed with a pilot at Lancaster where the Barrow portion was detached, though either would have caused some delay. There was also Saturday, 10th January 1959, when W251 appeared behind twin diesels 10201 and 10202.

BR diesels, in the form of EE Type 4s, appeared quite early on W251 compared to most other expresses through Oxenholme; Alec's first sighting being Crewe North's D226 on Saturday, 19th September 1959, at the start of the winter timetable (Alec's first recorded sighting of an EE Type 4 at Oxenholme was D219 on Saturday, 1st August 1959 hauling W110, the 9-00 am Perth–Euston).

Until the summer timetable commenced in 1958, W251's loco was routinely provided by Camden, with the usual handful of substitutions by Crewe North or Upperby locos, and the odd 'stray'. From then on, Upperby having acquired an extra half dozen Duchesses, it became an Upperby job as for the southbound counterpart W74. Upperby acquired its first EE Type 4s in June 1959 and, when the winter timetable came in, Type 4s from Crewe North initially appeared quite regularly, but Upperby Type 4s and Duchesses, with the odd 7P, continued to cover the lion's share.

Compared to other long distance expresses passing through Oxenholme, W251's timekeeping was both somewhat better, and less prone to variation between the seasons. Across Alec's more than 200 sightings over four and a half years, W251 reached Oxenholme on time or early on almost half of them, and was no more than five minutes late on another 20%. As was generally the case, timekeeping was better in the winter timetable periods, almost two-thirds of trains being right time or early in both 1958/9 and 1959/60, but the seasonal difference was much less marked. Winter 1957/8 was an exception with 20% of sightings more than 20 minutes late, this continuing from January right through to the beginning of May, when things suddenly got better. It was late July, over 40 sightings later, before W251 showed up over 20 minutes late again. Even in the worst of its summers, which for W251 was unusually 1959, the train reached Oxenholme, and doubtless then its final destinations, on time or early more than 30% of the time, and on no occasions did Alec see W251 more than 20 minutes late.

4. Stopping Passenger Trains

The local passenger service through Oxenholme that served travellers to and from smaller stations between Carnforth, Windermere and Carlisle comprised, year-round, some eight to ten trains each way on the Windermere branch and about four each way between Oxenholme and Carlisle.

Windermere branch

In a typical winter timetable period, all but a couple of the scheduled passenger trains called at all stations on the Windermere branch – Burneside and Staveley as well as Kendal. So even though several of these trains travelled much further south, even to Euston, and changed their spots, and lamps between Class B and Class A, en route, they were fair game for local travellers. Unfortunately, Alec paid far less attention to local trains on the branch unless they ran through, so records are scarce, but the short-distance services were normally handled by Oxenholme 2-6-4Ts on a few non-corridor coaches.

The service on the branch was strangely unbalanced: taking Winter 1956/7 as an example, in the Up direction on weekdays there were only three short-distance trains that travelled no further than Oxenholme or Carnforth, but in the Down direction there were seven or eight.

The first southbound service from Windermere was the 6-32 am, which ran through to Carnforth, calling at Burton and Holme, closed to passengers in 1950, to set down newspapers. It also called at Milnthorpe, and connected at Carnforth into a Barrow to Preston train. Next, at 8-10 am, came W204, the 'Club' train for Manchester followed at 9-25 am by a train of four corridor coaches, which were collected at Oxenholme by W74, the 8-30 am from Carlisle, and taken through to Euston.

Around 11 o'clock, W86 set off for Euston, calling at all the branch stations, and then on weekdays there was nothing until the 2-10 pm Windermere–Oxenholme, which connected into W282, the 10-55 am Glasgow–Manchester Victoria. On Saturdays though there was a 12 noon service to Lancaster, which also called at Milnthorpe: one for the shoppers perhaps?

In mid-afternoon, W220 departed at 3-23 pm from Windermere and ran to Preston, starting out as a Class B train but becoming Class A from Lancaster. In the winter timetable period the loco, normally an Oxenholme 2-6-4T, ran light engine from Oxenholme to take the train to Preston, but in summer, this train was extended to run through to Liverpool Exchange and the loco was usually a 'Black Five'. Alec's notes show that on Saturdays this was usually a Bank Hall loco but on weekdays 'Black Fives' from various sheds turned up.

There was a gap then until 5-45 pm when another local train departed for Carnforth where connection was made into W302, the 3-10 pm Workington–Liverpool. Both these trains also called at Milnthorpe. Then it was the final train of the day, W370 the 8-30 pm Windermere–Euston, providing a through service from Staveley and Burneside to London, but in this case eschewing Milnthorpe.

In the opposite direction, the first passenger-carrying train of the day to head down the branch from Oxenholme to Windermere was what was locally known as the 'Mail', the overnight 11-05 pm from Euston of which just a corridor brake composite and a passenger brake survived the detachment of Blackpool and Whitehaven portions to reach Windermere. Calling at Kendal before 5-30 am it didn't call at Burneside or Staveley, and unsurprisingly it didn't appear directly in Alec's notes, though it is said that in later years he would clamber onto the footplate at Kendal for a cab-ride to Windermere, and back with the loco's next duty, the 'Club' train W204, before going to work!

The passenger service proper began with the 7-43 am 'all stations' from Carnforth, calling at Oxenholme at ten past eight.

Stanier 2-6-4T 42457, an Oxenholme loco throughout BR days until the shed closed in June 1962, heads south between Bolton-le-Sands and Hest Bank with the 3-30 pm Windermere–Preston train in June 1959, so prior to the commencement of the summer timetable when the train would be extended to Liverpool Exchange. Formed of four corridor coaches the train is running under Class B lamps, which would be changed to Class A at Lancaster. CRA Pearsall Collection PEH339.

Burneside station looking towards Windermere with Stanier 2-6-4T 42457 starting away with an Up local from Windermere in the early to mid-1950s. CRA Mayor Collection MAY054.

Fowler 2-6-4T 42317, an Oxenholme loco from Nationalisation until October 1959, arrives at Windermere with a local passenger on Saturday, 4th August 1951. CRA Dendy Collection DEN104.

Fowler 2-6-4T 42301, another Oxenholme resident throughout the 1950s, departs from the branch platform with a late afternoon Down stopping passenger towards Windermere. CRA Mayor Collection MAY135.

Some 35 minutes later, another branch local left Oxenholme at 8-45 am, providing a connection out of the Down morning 'Parly', the 6-00 am Warrington–Carlisle. And just after 9-30 am there was another train down the branch, this being W279, the 8-15 am from Preston, which *inter alia* provided the loco for the southbound W86 at around 11-00 am.

There was almost a three-hour gap to the next service down the branch, another genuine local, which provided an onward connection at 12-20 pm out of W27, the 9-25 am Crewe–Perth. The loco for the 12-20 pm came light engine mid-morning from Windermere having taken an earlier service down the branch. Around 2 pm, travellers towards Windermere could avail themselves of another through train, W33, the 6-40 am express from Euston, which became a Class B service calling at all stations, including Milnthorpe. W33 called at Oxenholme at 1-53 pm on weekdays, but it was 2-10 pm on Saturdays.

Then just after 4 pm on weekdays, a flurry of five passenger trains in three hours headed down the branch, starting with a local leaving Oxenholme at 4-10 pm with no connecting service; on Saturdays departure time was 3-30 pm. Then at 4-39 pm there were more through-coaches from London, a four corridor portion that went up to London the previous day with W74 now returning as a portion detached from W251 the 10-40 am Euston–Carlisle.

Yet another short-distance local left Oxenholme for Windermere at 5-15 pm, again with no connecting service. Needless to say, with all these trains heading to Windermere during the day, something had to come back, and an ECS left Windermere at 6-00 pm, arriving Oxenholme at 6-22 pm. This then formed the 6-56 pm local back to Windermere, providing a connection out of W99, the 1-35 pm Euston–Perth. Hot on the heels of the 6-56 pm though came W55, the returning 'Club' train from Manchester, which left Oxenholme just eight minutes later at 7-04 pm. Running two trains so close together like this suggests passenger loadings for Kendal and Windermere on both must have been heavy; on weekdays the 6-56 pm galloped straight through from Kendal without stopping, leaving Burneside and Staveley passengers to follow on the 'Club' train, but on Saturdays, when the 'Club' train didn't run, the 6-56 pm obligingly stopped at all stations.

The final train of the day down the branch also provided a connection from the south. This was the 8-39 pm from Lancaster, which connected out of the Down evening 'Parly', the 6-00 pm Crewe–Carlisle and called at all stations to Windermere reached at two minutes to ten.

In summer, some additional scheduled trains appeared in the timetable, the detail varying from year to year. Some ran through to or from places further south including Crewe and Blackpool for example, but some were added just along the branch, and then of course there were frequent excursions also swelling the volume of passenger traffic along the line.

Oxenholme – Carlisle

The local passenger service between Oxenholme and Carlisle was a much more limited affair, and in the late 1950s, after leaving Penrith, it seemed to exist principally to serve Low Gill and Shap, as well as slightly enhancing Tebay's meagre service. There was just a single southbound local leaving Carlisle just before 2-00 pm, and, somewhat oddly, two returning northbound locals leaving Oxenholme in the late afternoon and evening.

The first train of the day to call at these wayside stations was the 6-10 am Carlisle–Crewe, pedestrian despite its Class A lamps, which served all three — Shap, Tebay and Low Gill. A couple of hours later Shap was further honoured with a call from W74, the 8-30 am Carlisle–Euston, as was Tebay. But Low Gill travellers had to wait for their next service until the afternoon local, normally an Upperby 2-6-4T on a handful of non-corridor coaches, which left Carlisle at 1-51 pm and called at all three stations before reaching Oxenholme at 3-23 pm. That was it for Shap going south, as the final service of the day, the 7-00 pm Carlisle–Warrington, called only at Tebay and Low Gill between Penrith and Oxenholme.

Going north, the 6-00 am Warrington–Carlisle provided the first local service, calling at Low Gill, Tebay and Shap. It was the end of the day before the next train stopped at Low Gill and Shap, the 5-00 pm returning local from Oxenholme to Carlisle, but Tebay was favoured by W27, the 9-25 am Crewe–Perth, which called just after 12-30 pm. And that was it for Low Gill, but a second evening local ran from Oxenholme to Carlisle at 7-20 pm, calling at Tebay and at Shap. Perhaps the stock was balanced in that there were four coaches on the southbound train but the northbound services comprised just two each. Where the extra loco came from, or returned to, is currently a mystery. There was one last service for Tebay as W397 the 6-00 pm Crewe–Carlisle called there, at least in the winter timetable and on summer Saturdays, at around twenty minutes to ten.

In summer, a few of the additional scheduled expresses running north and south through the fells would also call at Tebay, enhancing the service, and one or two also called at Shap and Low Gill. One southbound example was W76, which in 1957 was the 8-20 am Workington to Crewe via Keswick and in 1958 the 9-18 am Keswick to Manchester Victoria. Strange to say, in Summer 1959, W251, the mid-morning Euston–Carlisle, which ran year round, was apparently scheduled to call additionally at Low Gill, Tebay and Shap, and Alec seems to have regularly availed himself of this service to get to Tebay in the late afternoon for cab-rides on the Shap bankers, returning on W150, the 7-00 pm Carlisle–Warrington.

Express headlamps they may be, but the 7-00 pm Carlisle–Warrington was a stopping train in every way. Regularly hauled by a Warrington 'Black Five', 8B's 45354 climbs the 1 in 131 towards Wreay, under the footbridge by Newbiggin Hall south of Brisco, on Tuesday, 22nd July 1958.
CRA Leslie Collection LES0592. By kind permission of Peter J Robinson.

Lambrigg Crossing in the snow in 1955, possibly late February when Westmorland experienced heavy snowfalls and there was a famous snowdrift at Bleath Gill! Stanier 2-6-4T 42544 of Carlisle Upperby eases what will surely be the 1-53 pm Carlisle–Oxenholme west across the crossing towards Docker Viaduct.
CRA Mayor Collection MAY197.

LMS Stanier 2-6-4T 42664 (12A Upperby) approaches Scout Green crossing on the 1 in 75 climb from Tebay to Shap Summit with the two-coach 5-00 pm Oxenholme–Carlisle stopping passenger on Saturday, 27th July 1957. CRA Leslie Collection LES0431. By kind permission of Peter J Robinson.

5. Parcels and Perishables Trains

Parcels and Mail

Threaded into the flow of passenger trains through Oxenholme, and scheduled in the Passenger Working Timetable, were a number of long-distance trains variously carrying parcels, mail, newspapers and perishable products such as fish, meat and milk. As far as the parcels trains were concerned, this threading was far from seamless, for by the time the Down trains reached Oxenholme their invariable lateness was more readily expressed in terms of hours rather than minutes.

The parcels trains that Alec recorded most often, and probably sometimes confused, were W167, the 9-55 pm Willesden Junction–Carlisle and W367 the 12-30 pm Crewe–Carlisle. Both were heavy trains, but their habitual lateness possibly stemmed from their numerous station stops, which the other Class C trains rarely made, and once out-of-course they would constantly have to be dodged out of the traffic stream and the lateness would easily snowball.

Coronation 4-6-2 46257 *City of Salford* stands with a Down parcels in the branch platform. Alec's notebooks suggest this would be Wednesday, 5th July 1961 when he noted 46257, now a Kingmoor loco, on 3L07 parcels, formerly W167, the 10-00 pm Willesden–Carlisle. Booked to call between 9-18 am and 9-31 am, the angle and elevation of the sun suggests it has gone 11 o'clock and 3L07 is its customary few hours late. The signal is 'off' for the branch to allow the train fully into the platform, but after loading/unloading it will reverse back through the branch platform into the Down Loop south of the station before departing northwards. CRA Mayor collection MAY361.

After spending 40 minutes at Preston, and 20 to 25 minutes at both Carnforth and Lancaster, W167 was scheduled to call at Oxenholme typically for 15 minutes from around 9-15 to 9-30 am. To avoid bringing the main line to a standstill W167 would run into the 'Bay' platform normally reserved for Windermere trains to load and unload. Sometimes, the train had to park up in the Down Loop south of the station until the platform became free, reversing out into that loop again before resuming its journey northwards through the fells.

W167 raised eyebrows if it appeared less than an hour late, and it was sometimes mid-afternoon before it showed up. The average lateness over Alec's 40-odd observations was over two and a half hours. W167 was normally hauled by an Upperby loco, around half the time by a 6P Jubilee or unrebuilt Patriot, but on a third of occasions, mainly between mid-1958 and February 1959, it was just a Class 5, and more often than not a Crewe loco. By 1961 though, the Duchesses started to appear, a sure sign of the times.

W367 also made lengthy stops at Preston, Lancaster and Carnforth, and at Garstang and Catterall, and Milnthorpe too, but then rumbled straight through Oxenholme, supposedly at around 5-15 pm, to its last stop at Penrith. Timekeeping was somewhat less grim, average lateness across Alec's observations being barely an hour and a half, though it reached five hours on occasion. W367 was most likely to appear headed by a Crewe North loco, with an Upperby loco being a frequent alternative. Again Class 6 power was the most common, with a few 7Ps supplied by Crewe on occasions, and 5MTs handling about a quarter of the trains Alec noted.

In addition to these two, there were three other trains that Alec rarely saw as they ran in the early morning or at night. These were W305, the 11-20 pm from Manchester Exchange to Glasgow (often termed a newspaper train), W475, the 12-02 am Birmingham–Glasgow and W73, the 6-48 pm Crewe–Glasgow. By the end of the 1950s W363, the 10-25 am Crewe–Carlisle, started to run MSX as required, and became regularly scheduled by 1961. As Saturday night turned into Sunday morning, additional trains were run to rush the Sunday papers northwards, such as W151, the 7-20 pm SO Euston–Lairg (which was reputed to be the longest-distance through train in the country), W305, the 9-27 pm Manchester Exchange–Aberdeen and W379, the 10-40 pm SO Manchester Exchange–Carlisle.

Coming south from Carlisle, the parcels train Alec most frequently saw, as it ran in daytime, was W356, the 8-15, or in some years 8-35 am, Carlisle–Crewe, known to railwaymen as the 'Horse and Carriage'. Apart from taking some nine hours to reach Crewe, W356 was famous for having a particularly motley collection of stock and is said to have got its name from what it carried in the days before the internal combustion engine. It also stopped everywhere, including Shap, Low Gill and Milnthorpe, and on Fridays it stopped too at the closed stations at Southwaite and Grayrigg to pay the staff!

In Winter 1956/7, W356 stopped at Oxenholme for around 20 minutes from around 10-30 am, but, when the Caledonian started running the following summer, W356 was held for almost an hour until that had flown through at 11-16 am.

The only other long-distance dedicated parcels train south through the fells was W372, the 11-45 pm Glasgow–Willesden, which clattered through Oxenholme before 5-30 in the morning. There was, however, a long-distance southbound parcels train that actually started on the branch in the evening — W400, the 6-35 pm SX Kendal–Euston. This left Kendal very much as a full train, and a substantial proportion of the traffic came from the K Shoes factory in the town. In Winter 1956/7, W400 called for five minutes at Oxenholme, ten at Carnforth, 25 at Lancaster and the same at Preston, though by Summer 1961 the Oxenholme stop no longer happened.

The loco for W400 arrived in Kendal light engine after taking W33, the 6-40 am express from Euston to Windermere. Taking Alec's sightings of W33 on weekdays together with those of W400, the motive power up until the end of 1959 was most often a Preston loco, usually a 'Black Five'. From early 1960, it seems Crewe North took over the duty, though locos from a range of other sheds from Patricroft to Holyhead, and even Saltley on one occasion, appeared too. More often than not it was still a 'Black Five', but Jubilees and 7P Scots and Britannias appeared increasingly frequently, including 'foreign' engines such as 70042 *Lord Roberts* of Trafford Park on 16th March 1960.

In addition to the general parcels trains there were of course the famous Up and Down West Coast Postals, 'Travelling Post Offices' with letters being sorted en route, the stuff of the 'Night Mail' . . . 'crossing the Border, bringing the cheque and the postal order . . . letters of thanks, letters from banks, letters of joy from girl and boy'.

The Up train was the first to depart at 6-30 pm from Glasgow Central and rushed south through Oxenholme just after ten in the evening after picking up mail on the move from the 'click' at Penrith and similarly exchanging mails in full flight at Carnforth. The Down train, W157, didn't leave Euston for Glasgow until 8-30 pm and with 100 miles further to go didn't thunder through Oxenholme until around two in the morning.

Alec's sightings of the Postals were inevitably few but the motive power was generally Pacifics, from both Polmadie and Crewe North.

Britannia Pacific 70042 *Lord Roberts* climbs away up the 1 in 80 from Kendal across the Sedbergh Road bridge with 1A65, formerly W400, the evening Kendal–London parcels, probably in the early 1960s. CRA Mayor Collection MAY366.

Fish, Meat and Milk

Much perishable traffic such as fish, meat and milk was conveyed in fast, Class C trains scheduled in the passenger timetable. The main flows through Oxenholme were south from Scotland, and Cumbria in the case of milk. W392, the 2-45 pm FSX Perth–London Broad St fish train, passed through Oxenholme at around 9-30 pm, early enough for Alec to record it if he was out late. It always had a loco capable of fast running, most often from Crewe North, and frequently a 7P Rebuilt Scot or Patriot, though Alec saw 'Black Fives', 6Ps and even a Duchess take their turn. The other scheduled fish trains were night owls, rarely observed flying through, such as W362, the 7-20 pm Law Junction to Broad St, W374, the 7-35 pm Law Junction to Manchester Oldham Road, and W352, the 6-55 pm Aberdeen to Manchester Victoria.

Passenger-timetabled trains carrying meat and milk were less straightforward, changing over the years and sometimes conveying both, and meat trains also ran as Class C freights. For many years there was also a regular milk train to London over the Midland route, and in some periods the milk train over the West Coast route only ran as required. The principal West Coast route trains typically left Carlisle around 3-30 pm, later 4-30 pm. By 1961, for example, the main milk train had become 1A69, the 4-30 pm Carlisle–Willesden, running also as required on Sundays at the earlier time of 3-30 pm. In the late 1950s, the equivalent on Sundays seems to have been W284, typically leaving Carlisle for Euston at 3-35 pm, timetabled as a parcels train, but most often recorded by Alec as a milk, or sometimes a meat train. Both W284 and 1A69 would call at Milnthorpe when required to collect traffic from the Libby's Creamery.

Crewe South 'Black Five' 45108 crosses the junction approaching Oxenholme from the north in the mid-1950s with an Up afternoon milk train comprising two milk tanks and three parcels vehicles. CRA Mayor Collection MAY532.

6. Freight Trains

The lines through Oxenholme saw a steady stream of passenger, parcels and perishables trains passing through around the clock, yet interspersed among them were freights of almost every description. There would be sixty or more on weekdays, fewer on Saturdays, with still a considerable number on Sundays, leaving aside the numerous 'control specials' that were arranged *ad-hoc* to convey additional traffic as needed. While Alec's passion was for express passenger trains he recorded the freights too, though he made no attempt to note timekeeping, as scheduled times for freights were honoured far more in the breach than the observance. His particular way of recording freights used signal box bell codes rather than headlamp codes, so a fully-fitted Class C would be a 3-1-1, a Class E a 1-2-2 and the cokes and coke empties were 4-1s.

Taking the Summer of 1957 as an example, 30 or more freights each way headed north or south through the fells on a weekday, most of them pretty evenly spaced between 6-00 am and midnight with around four each way during the small hours. Unsurprisingly, the line being a major Anglo-Scottish trunk route, nearly three-quarters of these were long-distance freights, two-thirds being fully- or partially-fitted express freights of Classes C, D and E. The remaining long-distance freights ran as Class H 'through freights', with just a couple of Class F, unfitted express freights.

The shorter distance freights comprised on the one hand as many as ten timetabled Class J trains carrying coke, or returning empties, between Tebay, the staging point for the Stainmore route to County Durham, and Furness. Then the daily roster was completed by about half a dozen local freights each way, whether on the main line or the Windermere branch, running as either Class H or K.

The afternoon of probably Saturday, 12th April 1958, and Alec has ventured north of Tebay to Scotchman's Bridge near Greenholme to capture Edge Hill 'Black Five' 45249 coasting down the gradient with an Up Class H freight, probably a Control Special, of pipes on bogie bolsters. Such trains of large pipes coming south from Scotland were a regular feature of freight traffic at this time. CRA Mayor Collection MAY317.

Express fitted freights, Classes C, D & E

Staying with Summer 1957 as our example, almost all the express fitted freights running north or south through the fells started or finished in one of the Carlisle yards. At this time every one of the southbound freights from Carlisle started from Upperby, their wagons being ferried there in the main by one of the many trip freights that shuffled daily between the various Carlisle yards before the New Yard opened at Kingmoor in 1963.

Northbound express freights almost all terminated in Carlisle, mainly at Viaduct Yard or the 'old' Kingmoor Down Sidings. The 12-15 am Ribble Sidings and 7-40 am Crewe Class Es, however, ran round the curve from Upperby to London Road Yard, and the 12 noon Class E from Walton Old Junction ran through to Canal Yard. The exceptions were three crack northbound Class C fully-fitted freights that continued beyond Carlisle, these being the 8-45 am Oxley–Law Junction, 1-10 pm Broad St–Glasgow Buchanan St and the 2-40 pm Camden–Buchanan St.

An unidentified LMS Stanier 5MT 2-6-0 hauls a Down Class C freight past Oxenholme No. 2 signal box at the south end of the station. An LMS 6P Jubilee 4-6-0, probably 45582 *Central Provinces* stands on coaches in the branch platform, most likely 1A34, formerly W86, the 11-05 am Lakes Express from Windermere to Euston. Probably Wednesday, July 5th 1961. CRA Mayor Collection MAY362.

Bank Hall Jubilee 45698 *Mars* was a frequent sight at Oxenholme, especially in summer when Liverpool–Scotland expresses were running separately. But here, crossing Docker Viaduct on the glorious morning of Thursday, 30th April 1958, she's been rostered to a Down Class C goods, and is banked in the rear. Records show that 45698 emerged from Works just the previous day after a Non-Classified (Engine-only) repair, which probably explains the pristine front end with a less than sparkling cab side and a distinctly grubby-looking tender. CRA Mayor Collection MAY287.

The express freights that ran north through Oxenholme to Carlisle started at various points from Crewe northwards, including Edge Hill, Walton Old Junction and Birkenhead on Merseyside, Liverpool Road in Manchester, St Helens, Warrington, several from Bamfurlong Sidings in Wigan and a lone example from Ribble Sidings in Preston.

Southbound, three express freights from Upperby ran beyond Crewe: the 4-38 pm Class C to Willesden, the 4-05 am Class D to Sudbury Junction and the 5-15 am Class E to Bushbury Junction. Otherwise, such freights from Upperby ran to a similar range of destinations in the Manchester/Liverpool/Crewe triangle from where the northbound freights started, including Liverpool Road, Edge Hill, Ravenhead in St Helens, Winwick Quay north of Warrington, Ince Moss in Wigan and Basford Hall and Gresty Lane in Crewe.

Most freights, even most Class Cs, were noted by Alec wholly anonymously simply as Up or Down 3-1-1s, or 1-2-2s. Notable exceptions were the crack Class Cs, the 8-45 am Oxley–Law Junction, sometimes a feature of his early Saturday afternoons, plus the 1-10 pm Broad St and the 2-40 pm Camden, both to Buchanan St, which he often saw clattering north in the late evening, along with the 6-24 pm Edge Hill to Kingmoor (SX) or Viaduct Yard (SO) Class D.

Stanier 5MT 2-6-0 42951 of Aston glides down from Grayrigg across Docker Viaduct and approaches the road bridge No. 83 at Docker with an Up Class E freight in the mid- to late-1950s. CRA Mayor Collection MAY276.

Such was the routine daily pattern of express freights through Oxenholme, but there were also multiple northbound paths, which were used by banana trains from Garston on Merseyside as and when required. They ran as Class C freights on fast schedules, though it seems the return of the banana empties was arranged *ad hoc*. In Summer 1957 these paths were at 11-36 am SX, 12-33 pm FSX, 2-00 pm FO, 4-00 pm and 4-30 pm SX and 6-15 pm FSX from Garston, all running to Viaduct Yard except where the Working Timetable is coy about the particular destination point in Carlisle.

Unfitted long-distance freights

There were typically around ten unfitted long-distance freights each way rattling along the main line through Oxenholme. Going south, all started from Upperby Yard, Class H freights running to destinations such as Winwick Quay north of Warrington, Ince Moss south of Wigan and Basford Hall and Gresty Lane in Crewe. There were also two Up Class F freights, which were unfitted, but ran to faster timings, because their formation was more predictable, being block loads or just trains of empties. They ran to Wallerscote (Northwich) and Weaste in Salford.

Going north, Class H freights ran from Bamfurlong, Bescot (Walsall) and Ordsall Lane in Manchester; the destination yards again being Viaduct, Kingmoor sidings and London Road.

Unrebuilt Patriot 4-6-0 45543 *Home Guard* climbs through Docker bridge (No. 83) with a Down Class H freight, probably in Spring 1958.
CRA Mayor Collection MAY346.

Mineral trains – Class J

Unlike most railway routes across the country, no regular through coal trains ran on the line between Carnforth and Carlisle. But there was a substantial flow of coke from the Durham area, across Stainmore to Tebay, that was then brought down, *via* Oxenholme and the Hincaster Junction to Arnside branch, to the Furness area for iron and steel-making.

Weekdays saw as many as five trains scheduled daily with a corresponding flow of empties back to Tebay, though it's not clear how many of these ran regularly in practice. In Summer 1957, these ran to and from Lindal Ore Sidings with the exception of the 10-08 am SX (9-47 am SO) from Tebay, which ran through to Barrow.

When Alec first started recording the passage of these trains, they were primarily hauled by LMS 4F 0-6-0s based for the purpose at Tebay, though 4Fs from Barrow were regularly to be seen as well. But, in early 1957, Tebay acquired the first of its Ivatt 4MT 2-6-0s, in the shape of 43028, 43029, and 43035 soon followed by 43011, and these started to monopolise the coke trains.

No. 43028 was the loco involved on 30th January 1960 when Alec started what became a favourite Saturday afternoon routine, heading off to Tebay early afternoon in order to ride in the cab of the 3-00 pm Tebay–Lindal coke train, returning to Tebay with the empties in the early evening.

Tebay 4F 0-6-0 44469 climbs under the A685 road bridge between Hay Fell and Docker with the 4-25 pm Lindal–Tebay coke empties on Monday, 25th April 1955.
CRA Pearsall Collection PEJ108.

Grayrigg, the summit of the climb from Oxenholme, had staggered Up and Down loops much used to stow freights out of the way of the stream of expresses. The station closed in February 1954. Ivatt 4MT 2-6-0 43028 has the road south from the ex-LNW lower quadrant starter and moves the 2-45 pm Tebay–Lindal coke, with a motley collection of wooden- and steel-bodied hoppers, slowly out of the loop. Tuesday, 8th April 1958.
CRA Pearsall Collection PEK208.

Local freights

Another Oxenholme Fowler 2-6-4T resident throughout the 1950s, No. 42313, starts a Down freight for the Windermere branch out of Oxenholme Down loops and under the Old Hutton road bridge in the mid- to late-1950s. The sheeted high goods may well be carrying imported wood pulp for Croppers' paper mill at Burneside. CRA Mayor Collection MAY122.

Freights serving local stations on the routes from Carnforth to Windermere and Tebay ran under both Class H and K lamps. On weekdays, on the main line, the first to call at Oxenholme was a southbound Class H freight, the 4-35 am from Upperby to Carnforth, which was booked to call from 7-29 am to 7-55 am.

First to appear in the Down direction was a 9-35 am SX Carnforth–Oxenholme trip freight, which arrived at 11-46 am, presumably shunted for quite a time, and departed back south at 1-50 pm, initially as far as Milnthorpe. It later continued at 3-25 pm back to Carnforth.

The final local freight of the day on the main line was an evening Class H freight from Carnforth to Tebay at 7-00 pm, which called at Oxenholme. It returned from Tebay at 10-37 pm calling again at Oxenholme and not leaving to return to Carnforth until nearly midnight.

On the Windermere branch the first freight was the 6-20 am Carnforth to Windermere Class H, the loco of which seems to have spent the morning making a couple of trips up and down the branch before returning south in the early afternoon. Arriving at Oxenholme at 6-59 am, the freight departed at 7-25 am calling at Kendal, where it dropped a variety of traffic, then Burneside, leaving coal and empty vans for the paper mill, and Staveley, again leaving coal, before arriving in Windermere at 9-51 am. It seems it then returned at 11-38 am as a Class K freight to Kendal, again calling at both Staveley and Burneside. After 35 minutes in Kendal, it headed back at 1-15 pm to Burneside to collect vans of paper products and empty coal wagons. It finally departed back to Carnforth at 1-50 pm, stopping again for 45 minutes in Kendal, and calling at Milnthorpe if traffic so required.

Around 8-15 am, the Kendal shunt engine Target 85 ran light from Oxenholme to shunt for the morning. It returned to Oxenholme banking the returning morning freight, 1-50 pm from Burneside. This stopped at Kendal on the Up line, the shunt engine attaching traffic from Kendal to the rear and banking the freight up the gradient to Oxenholme.

There was also a late morning trip at 11-30 am from Oxenholme to Kendal. The loco then returned light engine, before the afternoon branch freight came on the scene. This left Carnforth for Burneside at 1-06 pm, again as a Class H, calling at Oxenholme for an hour and a quarter, then Kendal for a similar time before arriving in Burneside at 4-35 pm. There was a prompt return from Burneside at 4-45 pm, but 45 minutes were spent at both Kendal and Oxenholme en route so Carnforth was not reached until 7-44 pm.

Carnforth 4F 0-6-0 44510, which sported a tender fitted with a snow cover for snowplough duty, pulls an Up Class H returning branch freight through the branch platform in 1953/4.
CRA Mayor Collection MAY140.

7. A Peak Summer Saturday at Oxenholme

While the Caledonian, the declared elite, if not the most venerable, of Anglo-Scottish expresses, was evidently Alec's favourite train, his favourite days must surely have been peak summer Saturdays when the railway was hectically busy with express passenger trains.

On such days, trains that in winter ran as a single train with many portions mushroomed into several separate trains, each of full length, and reliefs were added into the timetable to cope with peak passenger numbers that would otherwise overwhelm the scheduled services.

Then there were specials, destinations typically the seaside resorts of the Lancashire and North Wales coasts, but starting from points often unknown for scheduled services, taking holidaymakers for a week by the sea and returning them home the following week.

All this extra traffic had to fit into the normal carefully calculated and scheduled paths. To make things work at least tolerably, normal services were frequently re-timed by a few minutes or maybe more, generally involving somewhat longer journey times.

A southbound Special or Relief express in full flight, albeit in this case an Easter holiday extra. Upperby Jubilee 45593 *Kolhapur* gathers speed through the loops at Grayrigg at the start of the descent to Oxenholme with train W542 on Tuesday, 8th April 1958. CRA Pearsall Collection PEK205.

Alec was normally out and about watching and recording trains most Saturdays, though it seems he was required to work on Saturday mornings, so his observations typically started after lunch. But occasionally he managed a longer spell by the lineside, and his observations from one such occasion, Saturday, 2nd August 1958, provide a vivid illustration of the glories of a peak summer Saturday at Oxenholme in the heyday of BR steam. This was the closing week-end of the 'Glasgow Fair' holiday as well as the bank holiday weekend.

Alec spent the best part of eight hours recording trains, from 11 am to 7 pm, though with a break for lunch it seems, but the Special Traffic Notice for the day shows that many extra trains had already passed through Oxenholme during the night and the earlier part of the morning. Heading for Scotland there were four reliefs from Euston or Birmingham to Glasgow between two and four in the morning taking wandering Glaswegians back home.

Going south, it seems it was the turn of citizens of Renfrewshire and East Ayrshire for a summer holiday. By 4-30 am, two trains had already sped south from Kilmarnock to Euston and Blackpool, and there had been three Glasgow–London extras, two of them the famous 'Starlight Specials', which ran from Glasgow St Enoch.

From then on, the day's proceedings were coloured in the main by extras of one kind or another taking Scots home from the seaside, or perhaps from further afield. By the time Alec made his first note just after 11 am two specials had already headed into the fells from Blackpool Central. These were bound for Glasgow St Enoch and Dundee West respectively, and a third, from Morecambe to Glasgow Central, was already descending the Petteril Valley towards Carlisle.

After he'd noted Crewe North Jubilee 45624 *St. Helena* near Kendal on W204, Alec's first sighting of the day at 11-04 am was Bank Hall Jubilee 45698 *Mars* on another train from the Lancashire Coast, C881, a relief from Southport to Glasgow Central. First on the Up side at 11-17 am was Upperby's problem child, unrebuilt Patriot 45508, on W547, another southbound extra from Kilmarnock to Blackpool Central. At the same time Upperby shedmate Patriot 45504 *Royal Signals* was pulling into the branch platform with the Lakes Express, W86, the 10-50 am from Windermere to Euston.

No sooner would the 'Lakes' have been clear than C390, the 9-15 am Liverpool Exchange / 9-10 am Southport Chapel Street to Glasgow Central, pounded north at 11-23 am. It was hauled by the splendid combination of Kingmoor 'Crab' 2-6-0 42834, piloting a Perth 'Black Five', 45465, returning north after some earlier foray into England. Close on their heels was another of the double-headers that were a frequent feature of this busy day — C384, the 9-30 am Manchester Victoria to Glasgow Central, behind a pair of Newton Heath locos, 'Black Five' 44895 and Jubilee 45635 *Tobago*.

Back on the Up, the first of the Renfrewshire holiday trains flew south — W548 from Paisley Gilmour St to Blackpool North, six minutes early behind Upperby 'Black Five' 45197. Then C883, a relief from Liverpool Exchange to Glasgow St Enoch, went north behind 'Black Five' 45217, borrowed by Bank Hall from Liverpool's Brunswick MPD it seems. C883 was 22 minutes late, while close behind was another 'Black Five', Carnforth's 45097, running four minutes early on W515, the 11-25 am from Morecambe Euston Road to Glasgow Central.

That was just the first hour! The fun continued on the Up when Carnforth 'Black Five' 45193 arrived 25 minutes late at 12-11 pm on W134, the 7-32 am South Shields to Blackpool North *via* Stainmore and Tebay. She would have taken over the train at Tebay from NE traction, perhaps a couple of 76/77xxx Standard 2-6-0s, or Ivatt 43xxx versions.

Strangely missing from the northbound procession thus far was C386, the 9-43 am Liverpool Exchange to Edinburgh Princes Street, due to pass at 11-34 am. C386 must have been in some kind of trouble, for, when it appeared, Kingmoor Jubilee 45732 *Sanspareil* stopped out of course to get 'a sock on it'. The sock was duly provided in the form of Oxenholme's Fowler 2-6-4T 42313, probably at least to Shap Summit if not Carlisle, but the pair didn't depart until 12-14 pm, 40 minutes late, which doubtless rather gummed up the works on the Down side.

Meantime, the Up side still appeared to be running well and another Renfrewshire holiday special, this time W549 from Johnstone High on the western edge of Paisley going to Blackpool North, headed through three minutes early at 12-35 pm, behind Crewe North Rebuilt Scot 46151 *The Royal Horse Guardsman*.

By this time, however, the 9-50 am from Blackpool should have called on the way to Windermere, and three more northbound expresses should have headed into the hills: W241, the 10-02 am Warrington to Glasgow Central; W27, the 9-30 am

On the Tuesday after Easter, 8th April 1958, C386, the 9-43 am Liverpool Exchange–Glasgow Central was running as a separate train, seen here climbing past Lambrigg Crossing. Edge Hill 'Black Five' 45401 has a 'sock' in the shape of Fowler 2-6-4T 42364 of Barrow for assistance, presumably attached at Oxenholme in an out-of-course stop at some cost to punctuality. CRA Pearsall Collection PEK198.

Crewe to Aberdeen, and; C156, the 10-15 am Manchester Victoria to Workington *via* Penrith. But as the Down side was running around 40 minutes late Alec saw none of them before it seems he nipped off, somewhat unthinkably to us, presumably for some refreshment.

By the time he returned just before 2 pm he would also have missed C365, the 10-35 am SO Blackpool Central to Perth, and W271, the 11-05 am Blackpool North to South Shields and Darlington, as well as two specials from Blackpool North, one for Paisley Gilmour St and the other for Leven and Cardenden in Fife. On the Up side, W90, the 9-04 am Newcastle to Blackpool Central would probably have been running at least 25 minutes late behind W134; it hadn't appeared either before Alec broke for lunch, during which he also missed W28, the 9-10 am Glasgow Central to Blackpool Central, and the Up Royal Scot W96.

It seems the northbound traffic had caught up a bit while Alec was away, as Bury 'Crab' 42731 working W275, the 11-20 am Blackpool Central to Newcastle, drew to a stand for her Oxenholme stop only 20 minutes late at 1-51 pm. She would be replaced at Tebay, prior to the train heading over Stainmore. C382, the 11-15 am Liverpool Exchange to Windermere, departed 30 minutes late at 1-55 pm behind Bank Hall's 45210 while Carnforth's 45072 was only six minutes late on W517 Special, the 1-15 pm from Morecambe Euston Road to Glasgow Central, suggesting the cause of the delays was at least south of Carnforth.

Fowler 2-6-4T 42379, on Tebay's books for the summer timetable period in 1961, accelerates 1M54 (previously W90) the 9-04 am SSO Newcastle–Blackpool Central off Dillicar troughs and south towards the seaside. 42379 would have taken over the eight-coach train of LNER stock at Tebay from double-headed NE Region Ivatt or BR Standard Class 3 or 4 locos. CRA Buck Collection SBW039.

By a quarter past two there were signs of order being restored on the Down as 'Black Five' 45350 of Willesden pounded north two minutes early on C921, a relief from Blackpool North to Glasgow St Enoch due through Oxenholme at 2-12 pm. Indeed, such was the progress that W167, the 9-55 pm Parcels from Willesden Junction to Carlisle was allowed out into the traffic stream. W167 had been in the Down loop for goodness knows how long, given it was booked to leave nearly five hours earlier at 9-29 am. W167 was usually a very heavy train and on this occasion sported the odd pairing of Edge Hill Scot 46164 *The Artists' Rifleman* piloted by Longsight 'Crab' 2-6-0 42848.

All was certainly not well on the Up however, as next to appear was what was colloquially known as the 'Second Scot', W106, the 10-15 am Glasgow Central to Euston. Headed unusually by a pair of 'Black Fives', 45254 of Longsight and Crewe North's 45373, they were 37 minutes late going through at 2-20 pm.

Over on the Down side, W33, the 6-40 am Euston to Windermere, arrived 21 minutes late at 2-25 pm behind Upperby 'Black Five' 45259. This train collected a portion from Leeds, which left there at 11-16 am as part of a through train to Barrow, travelling *via* Settle and Wennington to Arnside, where the portion was detached and brought up the Hincaster branch to Oxenholme. The 'Black Five' on W33 itself had clearly been doing stirring stuff to claw back time from the earlier delays, for Alec noted it was reported departing Preston 42 minutes late at 1-28 pm and had recovered no less than half of that by the time it reached Oxenholme after calling at Lancaster, Carnforth and Milnthorpe.

Incidentally, Alec made no record of the loco that brought in the Leeds portion, which serves as a reminder that in the background to the feast of express passenger traffic hurtling through the main platforms would have been the normal to-ing and fro-ing of local trains between Windermere, Lancaster and Carlisle that Alec rarely noted.

Next on the Up though was W282, the 10-50 am Glasgow Central to Morecambe and Manchester Victoria, which went through just four minutes late at 2-40 pm behind Newton Heath Jubilee 45701 *Conqueror*, piloted by 'Black Five' 45449 of Springs Branch. The Morecambe portion would be detached from the rear at Carnforth and taken down the single line from Hest Bank to Bare Lane. On summer Saturdays this train used the GSW route to Gretna Junction, which suggests the delay to the 'Second Scot' was either a problem on the Beattock route or a problem affecting W106 itself, which maybe explains the two 'Black Fives' rather than the customary 7P or 8P?

Five minutes later at a quarter to three, Crewe North Scot 46135 *The East Lancashire Regiment* hurried north 16 minutes late on W715, a relief from Birmingham to Glasgow Central, and close behind thundered the LMS pioneer diesels 10000 and 10001 with the Down Royal Scot, W63, nine minutes late on amended timings, just a couple of minutes later than normal.

Problems coming south over Beattock, whether of W106's making or not, were maybe responsible for W110, the 9-00 am Perth to Euston, being 47 minutes late, eventually flying south far behind W282 at nearly 3 pm instead of well ahead of it soon after 2 pm. It was again unusually hauled, by Polmadie's 46231 *Duchess of Atholl* rather than the expected Upperby or Camden 7P or 8P. Polmadie Duchesses were rare visitors to Upperby, more usually turning back at Kingmoor or Crewe on a Glasgow job. Being a through working from Carlisle to Euston, it's anyone's guess where she ended up on this day!

Over on the Down side W67, the 11-15 am Birmingham to Glasgow Central hurried north just nine minutes late, perhaps a small enough deficit to be regained before Carlisle, given some flying on the descent from Shap, but as always dependent on the state of congestion around Citadel station itself. W67 had unexpected traction too: it was a Polmadie loco as usual during the summer, but instead of a Duchess or Princess Royal it was one of their Britannias, 70053 *Moray Firth,* daily visitors on the Glasgow–Lancashire services, but unusual sights on the Birminghams.

Inevitably, Bank Hall Jubilee, 45717 *Dauntless*, was similarly well down on W432, the 10-55 am Glasgow Central to Liverpool, passing at 3-09 pm, 42 minutes late, whilst sister loco, Crewe North Jubilee 45630 *Swaziland*, maintained the respectable state of affairs going north on the 11-25 am Birmingham to Edinburgh Princes Street, again passing nine minutes late at 3-15 pm.

Four minutes later another Scotland to Lancashire express rushed through south, W284, the 11-10 am Edinburgh to Liverpool and Manchester, being 31 minutes late behind Kingmoor's 44877. Following on behind, there trundled a light engine, Carnforth's 45306, returning from Tebay to Carnforth or maybe Preston after working W271, the 11-05 am Blackpool North to South Shields, which had gone north while Alec was away at lunch.

If things had settled on the northern part of the West Coast main line going north, it seems there was still a legacy of earlier delays affecting at least some trains from further south. Patriot 45550 of Edge Hill was running a massive 54 minutes late on W681, a relief from Euston to Glasgow Central, due at 2-36 pm. And delays were still affecting trains from the line over Beattock; W270, the 7-35 am Aberdeen to Manchester Victoria, double-headed by Upperby Patriot 45524 *Blackpool* piloted by Newton Heath's 44895 shuddered to a halt 32 minutes late for its Oxenholme stop at 3-38 pm.

With the Aberdeen still in the station, Camden Scot 46168 *The Girl Guide* pounded through northbound, just 22 minutes late at 3-38 pm on W57, the 10-10 am Euston to Glasgow Central 'Second Scot'. Indeed, things were looking distinctly brighter on the Down, and W65, in winter a Carlisle–Perth train but today extended back as the 10-20 am from Euston, followed

With all the down-at-heel air of a miscreant, whether causing trouble that day or not, a very grubby Coronation 4-6-2 46246 *City of Manchester*, the last of the class to retain the sloping 'semi' smokebox, heads W106 the 'Second Scot', 10-05 am Glasgow–Euston passenger, a motley rake of 16 coaches, down from the Sedbergh Road bridge past milepost 20 and towards Oxenholme station. Saturday, 1st August 1959. CRA Pearsall Collection PEK710.

Another Scotland–Liverpool train running separately on a summer Saturday. Crewe North 'Black Five' 45311 and Bank Hall Jubilee 45719 *Glorious* double-head 1M27, formerly, W432, the 10-50 am Glasgow Central–Liverpool Exchange express, into the deep cutting under Rowell Lane, north of Milnthorpe on 22nd July 1961. CRA Pearsall Collection PES383.

An unidentified unrebuilt Patriot leaves behind the loops at Burton & Holme and sets herself for the climb ahead with W681, the 1-00 pm Euston–Glasgow relief express on Friday, 31st July 1959. CRA Pearsall Collection PEK705.

'Black Five' 45026 of Springs Branch begins the climb to Shap Summit just north of Tebay with C860, a Down Special express passenger in the early to mid-1950s. CRA Mayor Collection MAY333.

only 13 minutes late behind Edge Hill Rebuilt Patriot 45534 *E. Tootal Broadhurst*. There were no such bright signs on the Up side yet though and Newton Heath Jubilee 45710 *Irresistible* ran through 38 minutes late at 3-55 pm on Special 550, a relief from Glasgow Central to Manchester and Liverpool. Then Alec recorded a train off the branch for a change as Bank Hall's 45210 worked W220, the 3-15 pm Windermere to Liverpool Exchange, near enough right time it appears.

Recovery on the Down was now looking to be complete as Polmadie's 72001 *Clan Cameron* headed into the hills with C392, the 2-15 pm Liverpool Exchange to Glasgow Central, bang on time at 3-57 pm. There were signs of improvement on the Up too as Newton Heath Jubilee 45700 *Amethyst* hurried through at 4-00 pm, just 22 minutes late with W434, the 12 noon Glasgow Central to Manchester. Five minutes later the second train in a row went north right time, C400, the 2-00 pm Manchester Victoria to Glasgow Central and Edinburgh Princes St, behind Newton Heath 'Black Five' 44890, obviously doing a sterling job.

Then, for the first time all day, Alec recorded a freight. Tebay's Ivatt 2-6-0 43029 clattered through on an 'Up 1-2', probably the 3-00 pm coke train from Tebay, which ran to Lindal *via* the branch from Hincaster Junction to Arnside. Perhaps there was already a gleam in his eye, for less than 18 months later this train was to become his regular Saturday afternoon cab-ride, coming back to Tebay in the evening with the empties.

For some reason, Upperby 'Black Five' 45412 on W277, the 2-05 pm Blackpool North to Glasgow Central, which called at Oxenholme, broke the pattern of right time running on the Down, departing 34 minutes late at 4-23 pm. Otherwise, pressure generally seems to have been easing as Alec then noted Crewe South 8F 2-8-0 48655 on a Down fitted freight, and Carnforth 4F 0-6-0 44399 came in from Kendal on a freight off the branch, probably for Carnforth. Crewe North's 46249 *City of Sheffield* restored order going north on W126, the Up Midday Scot, just six minutes late at 4-39 pm, and Workington 4F 0-6-0 44157 went down the branch light engine, clearly on a mission of some kind to Windermere.

But then it was back to late running as Upperby Scot 46165 *The Ranger (12th London Regt.)* rolled in 30 minutes late at 5-00 pm on W251, the 10-40 am Euston to Carlisle, another through engine working, having dropped a Barrow portion at Lancaster. The delays persisted as two specials followed, returning holidaymakers to Glasgow from the North Wales coast. Crewe North Scot 46134 *The Cheshire Regiment* was 35 minutes late on W632 from Colwyn Bay to Glasgow, and Upperby's 45329 piloting Camden Jubilee 45601 *British Guiana* on W636 from Llandudno to Glasgow Central was doing slightly better, powering though six beats to the bar 18 minutes late at 5-30 pm. The disappointing pattern continued as Crewe North Scot 46161 *King's Own* arrived 19 minutes late at 5-41 pm on W121, the Down Lakes Express. The Windermere portion would be left in the platform while *King's Own* took the Keswick and Workington portion as far as Penrith before continuing light engine for R&R at Upperby MPD.

Things were still no better on the Up, and W484, the 12-15 pm Perth to Euston, was well down behind Upperby's 46244 *King George VI*, being 49 minutes late at 5-45 pm. W128, the 1-45 pm Glasgow Central and Edinburgh to Manchester and Liverpool, which called at Oxenholme, screeched to a stand 25 minutes late at 5-55 pm, double-headed by Blackpool Jubilee 45580 *Burma* piloting Polmadie's 72003 *Clan Fraser*. In the winter timetable, this train was the humble 4-10 pm Carlisle to Preston local.

Then, the skies cleared, and controllers' brows were doubtless unfurrowing a little, as Crewe North Scot 46138 *The London Irish Rifleman* was able to roar through two minutes early at 6-05 pm on W143, the 1-05 pm Euston to Glasgow unadvertised relief to the Down Midday Scot. On the Up, there was even room for a freight, at least a fully-fitted Class C in the hands of Upperby Patriot 45551. The calm of the evening continued as Crewe North's 46248 *City of Leeds* was just eight minutes late at 6-24 pm with W97, the Down 'Midday' proper, all the way from Euston, and Jubilee 45642 *Boscawen* of Newton Heath was likewise doing well on C402, the 4-25 pm Liverpool Exchange to Glasgow Central, passing two minutes late at 6-30 pm.

As the tensions of the day unwound, there was even time for an unfitted freight, 4F 0-6-0 43931 of Stourton rolling through on the Down, presumably to Tebay, and the

'Black Five' 44876, which was an Aston loco from 1951 to 1965, heads a Down express passenger W?23, very probably a Special or relief, round the curve through Low Gill station. CRA Mayor Collection MAY342.

purpose of 44157's mission was revealed. The Workington loco returned from Windermere with an ECS. Tebay's Ivatt Class 4 2-6-0 43029 returned from Lindal with the empty coke hoppers to Tebay, whilst the Up line witnessed the unusual sight, for 1958, of Edge Hill's 46114 *Coldstream Guardsman* on a freight, albeit an at least partly-fitted Class D.

As Alec's day drew to a close, things had clearly settled too on the Up as Newton Heath Jubilee 45706 *Express* raced down from the hills and off towards Carnforth pretty much right time with W442, the 1-57 pm Gourock to Manchester Victoria CTAC Scottish Tours Express due through at 6-51 pm.

It only remained for a familiar friend, Upperby Scot 46136 *The Border Regiment,* working through from Euston with W99, the 1-20 pm Euston to Perth, to draw to a stand dead on 7 pm, a forgivable nine minutes late, before Alec stowed away his notebook and headed for home.

Oh, that we could witness a day of such things again!

A Newton Heath Jubilee with a Fowler tender, probably 45700 *Amethyst* or 45712 *Victory,* approaches Lambrigg Crossing with Up express passenger W128/2, the second portion of the c.1.45 pm Glasgow/Edinburgh–Manchester/Liverpool, in the early to mid-1950s. CRA Mayor Collection MAY196.

Newton Heath Jubilee 45642 *Boscawen* speeds down the 1 in 75 past Scout Green signal box with an Up CTAC Scottish Tours Express, complete with headboard. Note the tall LNWR lower quadrant Up Home signal. Saturday 27th July 1957. CRA Leslie Collection LES0432. By kind permission of Peter J Robinson.

Acknowledgements

It has been a privilege to have been invited by the Cumbrian Railways Association to assemble the material for this publication, and a real pleasure to pull it together with the unstinted assistance of so many CRA members. Though the cover carries my name, and any errors or deficiencies are mine and mine alone, the text and many of the photographs are derived almost entirely from the painstaking work of two people sadly no longer with us — Alec Mayor and Paul Irving. Without them, such a publication simply would not have been possible. I do hope they would feel I have done tolerable justice to their work and their enthusiasm.

My particular thanks must go to Dave Richardson and to Mike Peascod for initially entrusting me with the task, for encouraging my evolving ideas and for supporting me in so many ways through to completion.

The finished product of course owes so much to Allan Jones, who has set the text and images, to Alan Johnstone and Guy Wilson who have produced the all-important track plan and maps, and to David Gibson for diligently re-scanning many of Alec Mayor's images to get the best possible from them. I am indebted to Ken Harper and Ron Herbert for reading through the draft text and their helpful suggestions for improvement. Thanks too to Mike Norris for his expert guidance on signalling matters, and Peter Smith for alerting me to the invaluable archive of Passenger Train Marshalling documents curated by the BR Coaching Stock group https://brcoachingstock.groups.io/g/main.

I'm grateful to Tony Jenkinson, Ewan Preston and my brother Roger Pickup not just for numerous conversations about trains around Oxenholme but for helping CRA re-discover Alec Mayor's original notebooks, which had been providentially scanned years ago by Chris Coates, the compiler and publisher of West Coast Sighting Sheets. And my special thanks to Chris and his group also for preserving and sharing the BR(LMR) Western Lines Special Traffic Notice covering Saturday, 2nd August 1958, which allowed many special trains featured in the final chapter to be identified.

Many sources on the worldwide web too numerous to detail inevitably contribute in one way or another during such a project, but I must acknowledge particularly the compilers of the BR Database site www.brdatabase.info whose pages have been a principal source of contemporary locomotive allocations, and Timetable World www.timetableworld.com for their invaluable collection of public passenger timetables.

Finally, my thanks to the many other CRA members, especially the organisers and contributors to the CRA Chatline, who have provided all manner of helpful insights during the progress of this publication: Peter Bacon, Ian Clemmet, Derrick Codling, Keith Fenwick, Richard Foster, Les Gilpin, Mike Hanson, David Hunter, Stephen Leece, Andrew Naylor, Howard Quayle, Tim Saunders, Donald Sills, Dick Smith, Nick Stanbra, Dave Stubbins, Philip Tuer, Peter White and Graham Worsnop.

Thank you again, one and all.

The Alec Mayor Notebooks, June 1957–1961

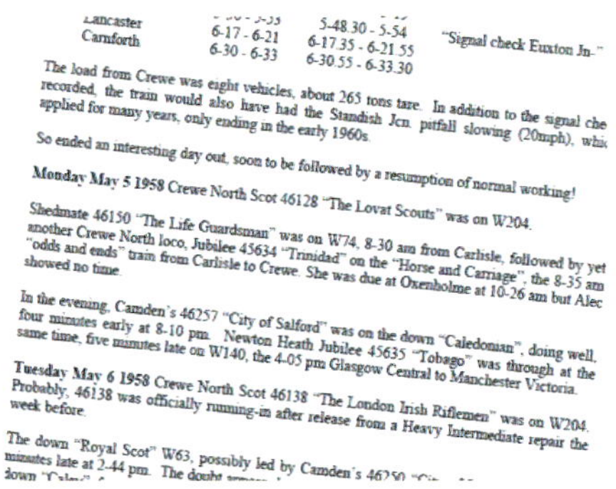

Lancaster		5-48.30 - 5-54	
Carnforth	6-17 - 6-21	6-17.35 - 6-21.55	"Signal check Euxton Jn."
	6-30 - 6-33	6-30.55 - 6-33.30	

The load from Crewe was eight vehicles, about 265 tons tare. In addition to the signal che
recorded, the train would also have had the Standish Jcn. pitfall slowing (20mph), whic
applied for many years, only ending in the early 1960s.

So ended an interesting day out, soon to be followed by a resumption of normal working!

Monday May 5 1958 Crewe North Scot 46128 "The Lovat Scouts" was on W204.

Shedmate 46150 "The Life Guardsman" was on W74, 8-30 am from Carlisle, followed by yet
another Crewe North loco, Jubilee 45634 "Trinidad" on the "Horse and Carriage", the 8-35 am
"odds and ends" train from Carlisle to Crewe. She was due at Oxenholme at 10-26 am but Alec
showed no time.

In the evening, Camden's 46257 "City of Salford" was on the down "Caledonian", doing well,
four minutes early at 8-10 pm. Newton Heath Jubilee 45635 "Tobago" was through at the
same time, five minutes late on W140, the 4-05 pm Glasgow Central to Manchester Victoria.

Tuesday May 6 1958 Crewe North Scot 46138 "The London Irish Riflemen" was on W204.
Probably, 46138 was officially running-in after release from a Heavy Intermediate repair the
week before.

The down "Royal Scot" W63, possibly led by Camden's 46250
minutes late at 2-44 pm. The doubt

The many thousands of detailed observations about trains, locos, timekeeping, and performance around Oxenholme and further afield, which have provided a unique source for this book, were compiled into a fascinating chronological narrative by the late Paul Irving, a career railwayman.

The complete text, enriched with loco allocations and some detailed annotations during editing by John Pickup, runs to some 200,000 words, and the compiled work can be purchased as a downloadable, searchable pdf from the CRA website: https://www.cumbrianrailways.org.uk

Photos on the back cover:

Upper: Around a quarter past eleven in the morning, between July 1957 and June 1958, possibly on Friday 14th March 1958, Alec Mayor's favourite train the Caledonian express rushes down from the fells to cross the junction with the Windermere branch at the north end of Oxenholme station behind Camden Duchess Pacific 46244 *King George VI.* CRA Mayor Collection MAY363.

Lower: Unrebuilt Patriot 4-6-0 45543 *Home Guard* climbs through Docker bridge (No. 83) with a Down Class H freight, probably in Spring 1958. CRA Mayor Collection MAY346.